LORD

Teach Me to Study the Bible in 28 Days

KAY ARTHUR

HARVEST HOUSE PUBLISHERS

EUGENE, OREGON

LORD, TEACH ME TO STUDY THE BIBLE IN 28 DAYS
Copyright © 2006 by Precept Ministries International
Published by Harvest House Publishers
Eugene, Oregon 97402

Arthur, Kay, 1933–
  Lord, teach me to study the Bible in 28 days / Kay Arthur.
        p. cm.
  ISBN-13: 978-0-7369-1603-5 (pbk.)
  ISBN-10: 0-7369-1603-2
  1. Bible—Study and teaching. I. Title.
  BS600.3.A79 2006
  220.071—dc22
                                2006010908

Printed in the United States of America

06 07 08 09 10 11 12 13 14 / ML-MS / 10 9 8 7 6 5 4 3

Contents

Before You Begin

Welcome to the world of inductive Bible study! Thank you for joining me on this exciting journey as we learn how to read and study God's Word, the Bible, and experience its life-changing power.

This is a very practical, hands-on, learn-by-doing book. The tools you'll discover are not hard to use. In fact, they are so easy to use that you are going to wonder why you weren't taught this years ago!

You can do it—you can study the Bible for yourself and understand it correctly. Anyone who can read can do it. And this is what makes this way of studying the Bible so wonderful. God has not reserved His Bible for the intellectually superior. Rather, He intends for all people, regardless of their intellect or education, to know and understand His Word.

The Bible text that we will use in this study is included in this book. You'll also find spaces in these pages to record your insights. All you need is a pencil, a pen, and some colored pencils for marking the Bible text. And don't forget to equip yourself with the most important tool of all—prayer! Pray that God will continue to whet your appetite for the truths in His Word. Ask Him to help you see the wonderful things He has provided for you in the Bible. Those are prayers He loves to answer!

Introduction

In 74 minutes, Lucinda would live, never to die again.

I was teaching in the Secured Housing Unit of the largest women's prison in the United States. From where I stood, I could see the silhouette of Lucinda's hard, flat, rail-like form through the small window next to the huge brownish orange iron door that locked her in. Everything about Lucinda—the pallor of her skin, her shaved head, and the vacant stare of her eyes—spoke of death.

Every fiber of my being—body, soul, and spirit—was focused on what I was doing. I knew without a shadow of a doubt that this unusual opportunity came about because of God, and I was there because the women needed to hear not my words but God's. Mine were the words of man; His are the words of life—divinely empowered.

I watched His words cut like a sword as I read and explained Romans 1 along with other scriptures. I saw the pain. In my heart I cried to God for her life, for liberation from sin and death, for a way to live behind razor-sharp barbed wire and monstrous walls that separated Lucinda from the beauty and solace of trees and gardens and ponds.

I thought about what life must be like, caged in that cell. The SHU housed the worst offenders—the most rebellious, most dangerous, most violent. The most desperate. Souls so angry, so frustrated, they thought they could fight the system and get away with it. Or they didn't care anymore—all that mattered was venting rage or getting revenge.

These were the walking dead, entombed in cold concrete mausoleums. Only a trip to the shower or the doctor brought them from their cell. Then they walked in chains. Everything— food, books, mail, medicine—left or entered their cell through a small metal trap door at the bottom of the brownish orange door.

I wasn't naive enough to think my God-ordained visit would spring open the doors of this prison for any of them. But I did know God could use it to roll away the stone that trapped them in their spiritual tombs and bring them from death to life. I knew if God would give them ears to hear and hearts to believe, they could gain a true knowledge of God that would bring power and divine purpose to their lives so they could live anywhere—in the prison or out—as overcomers of any and every circumstance of life.

In the course of my 74-minute presentation this precious lesbian, along with surprisingly many others in the SHU, all with stories of their own, passed from death to life. It was a glorious moment as I donned the required prison gear to protect my face and chest and walked to Lucinda's cell on the second level. Her brown eyes, swimming in tears, shimmered with light.

We talked. She truly understood. The old Lucinda had died; a new Lucinda had been born. No more anarchy. No more women. God would be her source of love and comfort and satisfaction. Yes, she would experience temptation and isolated acts of sin, but never again would she be sin's prisoner, sin's slave. Truth had set her free.

As I sit to write this book for you, dear reader, three years have passed. Lucinda's address is still the same, but she is not. Her feminine appearance, her hair, her hunger for and understanding of the Word of God, and her changed life all witness to her salvation. Lucinda passed from death to life—eternal life. He who began a good work in her will "complete it until the day of Jesus Christ" (Philippians 1:6). Lucinda is a brand-new creation. Old things passed away and all things became new, just as I taught from 2 Corinthians 5:14-21 that epochal night she heard the words of life.

Lucinda is in the process of being transformed by the "true knowledge of Him who called [her] by His own glory and excellence" (2 Peter 1:3), and because of that, she is able to live as more than a conqueror in the midst of what I consider the hardest and potentially most depressing of circumstances.

Lucinda is studying her Bible the way you are about to learn to study yours.

The question is, how did Lucinda get so messed up even though she had a religious background?

How does anyone waste a life?
Waste away?
End up without answers to the most common of life's issues?
Unequipped, unarmed, and unprepared to withstand the devastating seductions of the world, the flesh, and the devil? Believing a lie?

Let's see what God says as we cry out, "Lord, teach me to study the Bible in 28 days." All the answers are in His book, the Bible. If we know the cause of mankind's spiritual imprisonment, we can determine the cure.

WEEK ONE

How Critical Is Knowledge?

We are going to spend the first few days of our four-week adventure exploring the words of a prophet and the reign of a king. In the process, we'll try out some skills that will teach you how to study your Bible for yourself.

I am convinced God's message through the prophet Hosea is the same as His message to us today: It is absolutely essential for each of us—man or woman, young or old—to understand the importance and value of knowing the truth. In other words, you must know the Word of God, the Bible. And I think you believe it is important also. When you open the pages of the Bible, you know God has much more to teach you from its pages. And that's exactly why He has directed you to this book.

The purpose of *Lord, Teach Me to Study the Bible in 28 Days* is not to give you a lot of information on how we got the Bible, why it is structured the way it is, or how you can know it is truly the Word of God. All that is wonderful and enlightening information, but you can find that in many other great books. Besides, as the title of this book promises, we have only 28 days!

Therefore, my purpose is to teach you how to study the Bible

for yourself so you can discover truth for yourself. To intro-
duce you to some basic study skills that will open the Word of
God for you in an incredible, life-changing way. Because we
only have 28 days, I won't teach you everything I could, but I
promise that by the end of this book you'll be discovering truth
for yourself in a way that will transform your life. And if you
want to know more, I'll tell you where to go next.

When Jesus prayed for you (the Bible tells you God knew
you before you were ever born), He asked the Father to keep
you from the evil one by setting you apart through His truth.
Then Jesus, who cannot lie because He is the truth, made the
statement that God's Word is truth. You'll find Jesus' prayer for
you in John 17:15-17.[1] Let me quote it for you so you can read
it for yourself.

> I do not ask You to take them out of the world, but
> to keep them from the evil one. They are not of
> the world, even as I am not of the world. Sanctify
> them in the truth; Your word is truth.

The Bible explains in many ways throughout the Old and
New Testaments that it *is* the very word of God; not that it
contains His words, but that it is "My word...which goes forth
from My mouth" (Isaiah 55:11)! The words are recorded by
men using their own personality and vocabulary, but in God's
divine mystery, He superintended over the writers as He moved
them by His Spirit (2 Peter 1:20-21). God inspired (breathed)
the words, as 2 Timothy 3:16 says.

Let's take a few minutes *so you can see for yourself* what
God said through His messenger, Hosea, about the state of His

---

1. We know from John 17:20—"I do not ask on behalf of these alone, but for those
also who believe in Me through their word"—that this prayer includes all believers.
John the apostle was among the "these," and this is what he wrote under the divine
moving of the Spirit of God.

chosen people, the Israelites (later referred to as the Jews). In God's message to them, He has a message for us.

Hosea 4:1-3,6 is printed out below. I am going to ask you to read these verses more than once. The first time, simply read them aloud. Do it slowly so that you hear every word. Remember, these are God's words—so listen carefully!

1 Listen to the word of the LORD, O sons of Israel,
  For the LORD has a case against the inhabitants of the land,
  Because there is no faithfulness or kindness
  Or knowledge of God in the land.
2 There is swearing, deception, murder, stealing and adultery.
  They employ violence, so that bloodshed follows bloodshed.
3 Therefore the land mourns,
  And everyone who lives in it languishes
  Along with the beasts of the field and the birds of the sky,
  And also the fish of the sea disappear.
6 My people are destroyed for lack of knowledge.
  Because you have rejected knowledge,
  I also will reject you from being My priest.
  Since you have forgotten the law of your God,
  I also will forget your children.

Now read verse 1 aloud again. As you do, look for the answers to the following questions and record them by simply stating what the text tells you. This step is called *observation*. You don't need to use your imagination or make any additions or suppositions. Just state the facts of the text. In other words, see what the text says and record your observations.

- Who is speaking?

  Hosca

- To whom?

  the sons of Isreal

- Why? What is the reason these words are being spoken?

  No faithfulness or kindness or knowledge of God in the land

Great start. Now, read Hosea 4:1-3 again. This time, mark the word *knowledge*. If you have colored pencils as we suggested in the "Before You Begin" section, color *knowledge* green. If you don't have colored pencils, simply put a rectangle around the word until you get your colored pencils. You are marking a *key word*. A key word is an important word that helps you unlock the meaning of the text you are studying.

For the next 28 days you are going to color code important words—key words God uses to make His point. We use the color-coding process (rather than just symbols) because colors are easier to see, and too many markings can keep you from spotting key words easily.

Double underline in green the phrase *the land*. According to the book of Genesis, *the land* is the land God gave to Abraham, Isaac (one of Abraham's sons), Jacob (one of Isaac's two sons), and Jacob's descendants as an everlasting possession. (God changed Jacob's name to Israel, so Jacob's descendants are the 12 tribes of Israel.)

You've marked a few words in the text. It's colorful. But what's the point? Look at verse 2. Write down what you learn about *knowledge* from the setting or context of verses 1-3. Don't read any further until you do this assignment. If you truly want to learn how to study your Bible, you have to do your part. This is interactive—so now is the time to get active!

It seems to me that knowledge is God, or it is the Word of God. The Word of God, the ways of God are not being taught... knowledge. So bad things are happening.

Now then, since I'm not sitting right there with you (although I would count it a privilege to do so), let me ask you some of the 5 W's and an H (who, what, when, where, why, and how) about *knowledge*. See how many of them you have already answered strictly from your observations of Hosea 4:1-3.

- What's God's concern about Israel's knowledge?

   That there is none

- Knowledge of what or whom?

   God

- Where?

   in the land of Israel

- Who is saying this and to whom? (I know you have answered this once. It's a short answer—do it again so you get the impact.)

  Ultimately God to the Israelites

- What is happening because there is no faithfulness, kindness, or knowledge? (Answer this from verses 1-3.)

  swearing, murder, violence, stealing, bloodshed

Good. Now read Hosea 4:6 out loud. Mark the other two uses of *knowledge* in verse 6.

Now we are going to use the 5 W's and an H to cross-examine verse 6, or as I often say, to "interrogate" the text. Look at where you marked *knowledge*. As you examine the text, find the answers in verse 6 to these questions.

- What is God's concern about Israel's knowledge?

  the rejected knowledge

- Who is saying this?

  God

- Who is being affected?

  the children

- What have these people done?

  forgotten the law of God

- Once again, who are these people (see verses 1 and 6)?

  the Israelites

- What is going to happen to them as a result?

  God is going to reject them

- Who else will be impacted and why?

  the children

By the way, *languishes* (verse 3) means wastes away. Pretty sad, isn't it!

Now let's wrap up today by applying these truths to our lives.

God tells us in Romans 15:4 that what was written in earlier times was written for our instruction so that through perseverance and the encouragement of the Scriptures we might have hope. In the light of this, let's take what you have just discovered about *knowledge* in these Old Testament verses spoken to the people of Israel and see what you can learn.

What instruction in these verses in Hosea 4 will help you persevere in doing what God says, encourage you, and give you hope? This, by the way, is *application*. Application is studying God's Word and then ordering your life and your thinking in accordance with the truth of what you just learned or discovered. Let's answer a few application questions from these verses in Hosea. Some of them may overlap a little, but you don't need to write an answer more than once.

- When you studied *knowledge,* did you see anything that parallels our situation today? What was it?

  not learning enough about God

- Do you think people are being destroyed or ruined for a lack of knowledge of God? How?

  yes, God gives them over to their sin

- Has anything happened in your family, your state, or your country because of a lack of knowledge of God—of His Word? Is anything being ruined? What? (Remember, the Bible is the Word of God, so knowledge of God comes through His Word. His Word is the plumb line, the standard of all we believe.)

  missing the smile of God

- Has anything happened in your life as a direct result of your knowledge of God's Word—or your lack of knowledge of God? How has your knowledge of God helped you in a specific situation? What circumstances might you have handled differently had you known God's Word better? Jot down your answers.

- Do you have children? According to what you saw in Hosea, what might happen to them if you reject knowledge? Have you seen the effects of a lack of the knowledge of God in your country?

- Finally, has God touched your mind and heart in any way as you have observed and applied these four verses from Hosea? How? Write out your answer. Expressing yourself in words is part of the learning process.

depression

What Happens When You Don't Know God?

Today we are going to look at an account from the book of 2 Kings in the Old Testament. It's interesting, it's true, and it's right in line with our purpose as we begin this book—which is to show you how vital it is to know God.

Life can get distorted and out of whack when you don't know God. And you can't really know Him in truth apart from the Word of God. Look around you at the lives people are living. Find out how important the Bible is in their lives and how much time they devote to studying it. Notice the relationship between their knowledge of God and the way they handle life.

Read through 2 Kings 22:1-20 twice. You'll find the text on pages 147–149.

- The first time you read the chapter, pick any color except blue or green and color every reference to *King Josiah*. Mark all the pronouns (he, him, his, you, your) that refer to *Josiah* the same way, along with any other reference to him, such as *king*.

- The second time you read the chapter, put a green circle over every reference to time—the year in which something happens in Josiah's life—or you might draw an old-fashioned clock like this: 🕰.

Good. Now, briefly summarize what this chapter is about.

Josiah was a man who listened and submitted to God. God wrote that he would destroy Israel because it had forsaken God. But because Josiah repented before God... God promised that Josiah would not see that desolation.

The Word of God Lost
in the House of God

We're going to return to 2 Kings 22 today because it contains so much more for you, and I want you to be absolutely convinced of the importance of knowing God by knowing His Word and therefore knowing truth.

Yesterday when you read 2 Kings 22:1-20 and marked the references to King Josiah you undoubtedly noticed that this chapter is about finding the book of the law, which had been lost in the house of the Lord. In fact, you probably noticed quite a few references to the book of the law and to the house of the Lord. These are key phrases that will help us understand more about the chapter.

Therefore, here is your assignment for today:

- Color or underline every reference to *the house of the Lord* in blue. Mark all synonyms in the same way, as well as any pronouns, such as *it*. In other words, mark every reference to this house in the same way.

- Mark every reference to *the book of the law*—whether

it is simply called *it* or *this book* or *the words which you
have heard*. Color each reference green or draw this
symbol over it and color it green: 📖 .

When you finish, look at every place you marked *the house
of the Lord*. What do you learn about *the house of the Lord* from
marking these references? List your observations below.

*that it needed repair. Josiah saw
this need and made the request*

Now, look at the references you marked to *the book of the
law*. The Israelites (later known as the Jews) refer to Genesis,
Exodus, Leviticus, Numbers, and Deuteronomy as the *Torah*,
which is the Hebrew word for "law." Sometimes they refer to
the Torah as "the books of Moses" or even just "Moses," referring to the author. Christians have traditionally followed the
Greek translation of the Old Testament, which refers to the
same books as the *Pentateuch* ("five books").

What do you learn from marking the references to *the book
of the Law*?

*that it was not being followed.
the people needed "repaired" to.
because the people did not follow
the law they would be punished.*

Good job! This is interesting, isn't it? Have you seen anything at this point that confirms the value of knowing God and His Word? If so, write it out.

it seems that if we know God it will be good...? peaceful...? at least you will not have the wrath of God upon you.

this is hard... I do not wish to be scared into doing something.

Day Four

Seeking the Lord

Can you remember when you first read the Bible? I mean, *really* read it? I can.

I was raised in church and read portions of the Prayer Book every Sunday, but the Bible was a closed and boring book to me until I was saved at the age of 29.

Of course, the Bible didn't change—it has never changed and it never will. Rather, I changed. The Spirit of God took up residence in my body and gave me, as He does all believers, a hunger and thirst for righteousness. I now had an in-residence tutor just as you have if you are a true child of God, born of the Spirit, saved by faith in the Son of God.

Let's take a closer look at what 2 Kings 22 tells us about Josiah. Remember marking chronological references with a green circle—a clock? Let's see what you can learn from them. Answer the following questions by looking at those green clocks, starting with the first one.

- How old was Josiah when he became king?

  8

- How long did Josiah rule?

  31 years

27

- Where did he rule? (Double underline the name of the place with two green lines.)

  Jerusalem

- What was Josiah like?

  he did right in the sight of the Lord

- What happened in the eighteenth year of his reign?

  he, his people, found the book of the law

- Now, do your math! How old was he?

  $$\frac{\begin{array}{r}18\\8\end{array}}{26}\qquad 26$$

Let's look at an interesting cross-reference about Josiah and his reign in 2 Chronicles 34. Read the verses printed out below and do three things:

- First, color the references to *Josiah* as you did in 2 Kings 22.

- Second, mark the references to time with a green circle or clock.

- Third, double underline in green all geographical references (where something occurred).

2 Chronicles 34:1-8

1 Josiah was eight years old when he became king, and he reigned thirty-one years in Jerusalem.

2 He did right in the sight of the LORD, and walked in the ways of his father David and did not turn aside to the right or to the left.

3 For in the eighth year of his reign while he was still a youth, he began to seek the God of his father David; and in the twelfth year he began to purge Judah and Jerusalem of the high places, the Asherim, the carved images and the molten images.

4 They tore down the altars of the Baals in his presence, and the incense altars that were high above them he chopped down; also the Asherim, the carved images and the molten images he broke in pieces and ground to powder and scattered it on the graves of those who had sacrificed to them.

5 Then he burned the bones of the priests on their altars and purged Judah and Jerusalem.

6 In the cities of Manasseh, Ephraim, Simeon, even as far as Naphtali, in their surrounding ruins,

7 he also tore down the altars and beat the Asherim and the carved images into powder, and chopped down all the incense altars throughout the land of Israel. Then he returned to Jerusalem.

8 Now in the eighteenth year of his reign, when he had purged the land and the house, he sent Shaphan the son of Azaliah, and Maaseiah an official of the city, and Joah the son of Joahaz the recorder, to repair the house of the LORD his God.

Now then, look at the time phrases you just "clocked," and let's compare them with what you learned from 2 Kings 22.

- What new insights into Josiah's life did you find in 2 Chronicles?

that he began seeking God at the age of 16. He also started ridding Israel of false gods

- How old was Josiah when he began seeking the Lord?

  16

- How old was Josiah when he began to purge Judah and Jerusalem? *20*

- What did Josiah "purge"?

  Judah and Jerusalem ... the people?

- According to 2 Chronicles, why did Josiah do all this purging? *because it was right He was following God*

Are you thinking, "*Wow!*" I did when I saw this. I thought, "God, this is neat! I just learned something about Josiah that I wouldn't have known if I hadn't read 2 Chronicles 34." I gained new insight into Josiah by comparing Scripture with Scripture—checking out a cross-reference.

Tomorrow we will do another *wow!* But before we call it a day, what do you think about Josiah at this point—before he's in the eighteenth year of his reign, before he is 26? Write it down.

he is pretty amazing. that he followed God, he sought out God, he obeyed God

Day Five

Hearing God's Word

When you read 2 Chronicles 34 and saw that Josiah began seeking the Lord in the eighth year of his reign, when he was 16 years old, did you wonder, "Why? What caused this?" I did. I am always interested in the reasons people seek the Lord.

Look at the cross-reference in Zephaniah 1:1 below and see for yourself when God spoke to Zephaniah.

> The word of the LORD which came to Zephaniah
> son of Cushi, son of Gedaliah, son of Amariah, son
> of Hezekiah, in the days of Josiah son of Amon,
> king of Judah...

Zephaniah got his message from the Lord during the days of Josiah, son of Amon, king of Judah!

Zephaniah delivered a hard message. God was going to move in judgment—He was going to stretch out His hand against Judah and Jerusalem.

Jerusalem! Josiah lived there! The Lord was going to search Jerusalem and punish those who were "stagnant in spirit, who say in their hearts, 'The LORD will not do good or evil'" (Zephaniah 1:12).

And what did Zephaniah call the people to do? Listen to

Zephaniah 2:1-3. As you read it below, put a cloud like this around every occurrence of the word seek:

1 Gather yourselves together, yes, gather,
       O nation without shame,
2 Before the decree takes effect—
       The day passes like the chaff—
       Before the burning anger of the LORD comes upon
              you,
       Before the day of the LORD's anger comes upon you.
3 Seek the LORD,
       All you humble of the earth
       Who have carried out His ordinances;
       Seek righteousness, seek humility.
       Perhaps you will be hidden
       In the day of the LORD's anger.

When I read this I got goose bumps. I remembered what we read in 2 Chronicles 34. Look at it yourself. What in 2 Chronicles 34:3 relates to Zephaniah 2:1-3?

Josiah sook out righteousness

Once again I stood in awe at the Word of the Lord and how Scripture interprets Scripture. Zephaniah's message during the days of Josiah was this: "Judgment is coming, so seek the Lord." And Josiah listened!

Zephaniah's ministry is dated between 636 and 623 BC. (Remember, the calendar goes down until it reaches AD.)

• Josiah became king about 640 BC. In 636 Josiah would

have been 12. When Zephaniah's ministry ended Josiah would have been 25.

- 2 Chronicles tells us when he was 16 he began to seek the Lord. Perhaps Josiah gained the knowledge of God through the prophet Zephaniah and responded accordingly, seeking the Lord.

- When he was 20, Josiah began to purge Judah and Jerusalem.

Now then, for the sake of review, what happened in the eighteenth year of Josiah's reign—when he was 26?

the book of the law was found

And what happened then? We'll delve into that more tomorrow. Let me just ask you a question at this point, dear student. What has brought you to the point that you want to do a study such as this—to learn how to study your Bible, to seek the Lord?

to seek the Lord, to be in His presence, to surround myself w/ Him

Have you read anything this week that has encouraged you? What? *encouraged? no. afraid? yes*

Do you know that God says you will search for Him and find Him when you seek Him with all your heart? This was Jeremiah's message from God as recorded in Jeremiah 29:13 after the death of Josiah. Jeremiah was another prophet who prophesied during the days of King Josiah. He began in the thirteenth year of Josiah's reign! Josiah would have been about 21!

Day Six

The Impact of
Firsthand Knowledge

Hilkiah found the Word of God, which had been lost in the house of God. How did this impact a 26-year-old king who had been seeking the Lord—and doing all he could to follow Him to the best of his ability? What did a true knowledge—*a firsthand knowledge*—of God's Word do to Josiah?

Read through 2 Kings 22:3-20 again and list below what happened when Josiah heard the written word for the first time in his life.

- What did Josiah realize and why?

    that the people had not followed
    God and God's wrath was coming

- What was his response to the "words of the book of the law"? *He tore his clothes*

Have you ever wondered how God feels about certain things? Can we possibly know, or do we have to simply wonder? Beloved, there is no wondering to it. A careful study of the

Word of God, beginning with the Old Testament, will give you great insight, as 2 Kings 22 clearly shows.

Did you notice the phrase *the wrath that burns against this place* and the repeated phrase that talks about God bringing *evil on this place*? Read verses 11-20 again and underline these phrases in red.

- According to the text, why was this wrath, this evil going to come? *because Israel had not followed God*

- When would it come? Why this timing? Why not sooner? (This is an important answer—find it in the text!) *after Josiah had died. Because he trusted and feared God. God made a promise that He would not do it sooner*

When you read the last three verses of this chapter you know how God feels about Josiah's response to God's Word.

- What do you learn from these verses? *Josiah was tender and he was humble. This pleases God*

- What does this tell you about God? About His character, His ways? *that if we are humble God sees this and responds in kind "the smile of God"*

Now, what can you learn from all this for your own life? Is there any application for you to make? Any principles or precepts for you to embrace?

being humble to God and obeying Him is important. He will help me grow stronger and more stable as I trust and have faith in Him. As I rely on Him, He will give me happiness,

Day Seven

Responding to God

Have you ever wondered why America seems to have lost its founding fathers' reverence for God? You might ask the same thing about Judah and Jerusalem in the days of Josiah. Why was Josiah so shocked when he heard the reading of the book of the law? Shouldn't Josiah have known these things?

The answer is found in Deuteronomy 17:14-20, which is printed out below. It is a portion of the book of the law Josiah would have heard Shaphan the scribe read. Read this passage and mark every reference to the *copy of this law,* including the synonyms and pronouns. Mark them as you marked the references to *the book of the law* in 2 Kings 22.

14 "When you enter the land which the LORD your God gives you, and you possess it and live in it, and you say, 'I will set a king over me like all the nations who are around me,'

15 you shall surely set a king over you whom the LORD your God chooses, one from among your countrymen you shall set as king over yourselves; you may not put a foreigner over yourselves who is not your countryman.

16 "Moreover, he shall not multiply horses for himself, nor shall he

cause the people to return to Egypt to multiply horses, since the LORD has said to you, 'You shall never again return that way.'

17 "He shall not multiply wives for himself, or else his heart will turn away; nor shall he greatly increase silver and gold for himself.

18 "Now it shall come about when he sits on the throne of his kingdom, he shall write for himself a copy of this law on a scroll in the presence of the Levitical priests.

19 "It shall be with him and he shall read it all the days of his life, that he may learn to fear the LORD his God, by carefully observing all the words of this law and these statutes,

20 that his heart may not be lifted up above his countrymen and that he may not turn aside from the commandment, to the right or the left, so that he and his sons may continue long in his kingdom in the midst of Israel."

- List what you learn from these references.

that it is important to learn about God and stay in tune w/ His commandments

- List what the king was to do when he came to power.

he would write a copy of the law on a scroll in the presence of the priests

- Now, from what you've observed just in 2 Kings 22, why hadn't Josiah written his own copy of the law?

because he didn't know about it. His fathers had not been doing this

You will find 2 Kings 23:1-3 printed on page 149. Although the whole chapter is worth reading, we'll not do that. I simply want you to read these verses and see what Josiah did after he found the Word of God. His response to the Word of God stayed God's hand of judgment.

Oh, that the same thing would happen in our time! Oh, that we would find the Word of God in the house of God—beginning in us individually, for as a child of God your body is His temple, His house, and then in the church, His temple, the body of Jesus Christ (Ephesians 2–3). Oh, that grace and peace would be multiplied in our lives in the knowledge of God and of Jesus Christ.

This is my prayer for you, fellow student:

> that you may be filled with the knowledge of His will in all spiritual wisdom and understanding, so that you will walk in a manner worthy of the

Lord, to please Him in all respects, bearing fruit in every good work and increasing in the knowledge of God; strengthened with all power, according to His glorious might, for the attaining of all steadfastness and patience; joyously giving thanks to the Father, who has qualified us to share in the inheritance of the saints in Light (Colossians 1:9-12).

It is what Paul prayed for those in Colossae…and I am sure it is what our precious Lord Jesus Christ prays for us.

Now, Beloved of the unseen face but like heart, do you realize what you have been doing these past seven days?

You have been studying the Bible inductively. By *inductively,* I mean you have gone directly to the Word of God to discover what God says—to discover truth for yourself.

Reason with me. No one has told you what the text says, what it means, or how you are to think or live. Instead, by marking the text and by asking and answering the right questions, you have been observing, interpreting, and applying the Word of God. Congratulations! How proud I am of you—*and I really mean it!* You may not realize what you've been doing, but you've begun the process of learning how to study the Bible, how to discover truth for yourself. And it wasn't all that difficult, was it?

Tomorrow, as we begin our second week of study or day eight, I am going to explain what we've been doing, how you can develop the skills you've exercised and learn even more, and how to use them to study the very words of God book by book. It's going to be quite an adventure.

WEEK TWO

Day Eight

The Best Way to Study the Bible

The best way—not the only way, but the best way—to study the Bible is book by book. It's the way the Bible was written. God didn't lay out truth topic by topic; rather, His writers wrote out His Word for the most part in the form of books and letters (epistles). More than 40 men moved by the Spirit authored 66 books over a period of 1400 to 1800 years. The styles vary; some books contain mostly history, others law, biography, prophecy, proverbs, and poetry, but each book has a divine purpose . . . which is why God included it in His one Book.

The Old Testament of 39 books was complete before the time of Jesus Christ. Jesus quoted from it often and supported its veracity (truthfulness) right up to the time of His arrest and crucifixion (John 17:17). In quoting Deuteronomy 8:3, Jesus affirmed that the Old Testament contains the very words we're to live by (Matthew 4:4).

The New Testament affirms in many places that its content was divinely inspired. Paul wrote, "When you received the word of God which you heard from us, you accepted it not as the word of men, but for what it really is, the word

of God, which also performs its work in you who believe"
(1 Thessalonians 2:13).

Observation, Interpretation, and Application

Now, since the best way to study is book by book, we're
going to do just that. We're going to take apart the book of
Jonah. Jonah is a short but relevant book that will surprise
and delight you with its truths. You'll uncover its insights by
learning and practicing the simple but amazingly enlightening
skills of observation, interpretation, and application. These in
turn lead to transformation. According to Romans 12:1-2,
transformation of your mind, Beloved, enables you to discern
the will of God. Awesome! You're going to learn how to live a
life pleasing to your Creator. What peace and confidence that
will bring.

Observation is seeing—discovering—*what the text says.*
Before you can mine the truth from a passage, you must learn
to diligently observe it first so you know exactly what it says.
Was the author writing history? Poetry? A letter? Who are the
main characters? What locations are mentioned? Are some
words repeated?

Observation is the foundation for accurate *interpretation.*
Interpretation is discovering *what* the text means. What do the
words mean? What is the main point? What cross-references
might apply? Accurate interpretation depends on careful
observation. Both take time, patience, and prayer.

If you lay a weak foundation, your interpretation won't
stand; it will collapse on your head. If you lay a solid foundation, you'll have a safe shelter. The more you observe the text,
the more interpretation falls into place. So the first rule of
study is to observe, observe, observe!

Observation and interpretation will help you see what the text says and understand what it means, but to experience transformation, you must press on to *application*. Application is the process of conforming to the Word of God. How are you to live? To order your life in the light of truth? What are you to do? Asking these questions and then obeying is application. However, application is not always "doing something." Sometimes it is simply believing what you read—and if necessary, changing your mind to conform to the truth of God's Word.

Remember, whenever you open the Word of God you're studying the very *words* of God. I can't stress this enough, diligent one. Hang on His every word! His words are life (John 6:63)—pure inalterable truth, words so carefully chosen that God says they are like silver refined in a furnace seven times (Psalm 12:6).

God has inspired (breathed) the things He wants us to know—truths which are profitable, as 2 Timothy 3:16-17 says, for doctrine (teaching), reproof (showing us where we are wrong in our belief or behavior), correction (how to take what is wrong and make it right), and instruction in righteousness (how to live in the light of what *God* says is right) so that you and I and every other person who honors His Word will have His answers for every situation of life.

Doesn't it bring awe to your heart, Beloved, to know that you can find the solution for every situation of life in the Word of God—and that it will work if you'll live by it?

Second Timothy 3:16-17 are the best verses I know on what application is all about. Read the text and ask, what am I to believe, where am I wrong, how can I make it right, and how am I to live? This is application!

Where Do You Begin?

So where do you begin—what do you observe first? The rule of thumb is to look for the obvious—the easiest to see. And what's that? People! In historical, biographical, and prophetic books, begin with the main characters or people groups being addressed. In a letter, begin with its author and then look at its recipients.

Once you get started, you'll see that observation is much like peeling an onion, taking off one layer of truth to uncover another and another until you've seen everything there is to see.

Let's see how this works. You'll find Jonah on pages 149–154 of this book. We call these observation worksheets. Read through the first chapter of Jonah. Don't go further because I want you to watch Jonah's story unfold chapter by chapter just as it did in real life.

By the way, when you open God's book, remember to talk to the Author and ask Him to help you see and understand what He's saying, why He said it, and how He wants you to think and live in light of it. Remember, every book included in *His* Bible is stamped with *His* purpose.

Here's your assignment: Pray first and then read Jonah 1 and look for the main characters. Who's front and center in this chapter? When you finish, list their names below.

Now let's call it a day. Review what you learned about studying the Bible—observation, interpretation, and application—and then reflect on what you saw in the first chapter of Jonah.

As you discover for yourself what God is saying, begin to understand its meaning, and develop the habit of asking God how you're to think and live in the light of the truths you've studied, record what God is teaching you. This is where a journal comes in handy for many people. You may want to get in the habit of keeping one for every book of the Bible you study.

For this study I'd like you to keep a Jonah notebook to record your observations. You can also use this as a journal— to log personal things God shows you.

see journal

Day Nine

The 5 W's and an H

You read Jonah 1 yesterday and listed its main characters. For the next two days you're going to do something that will help you observe the text even better—"peel the onion" down another layer.

You're going to color code these characters for quick identification. So choose a color for *the Lord* and another color for *Jonah*.

Why these two? Because they're the most significant and prominent characters in chapter 1. As you saw, it's all about God and Jonah. The other characters, the captain of the ship and the sailors, are important but only in relationship to the Lord and Jonah. We'll look at them later.

- Read through chapter 1 and color every noun, pronoun, and synonym that refers to *the Lord* or *Jonah*. If you're stuck thinking about which colors, you can use yellow for *the Lord* and light blue for *Jonah*.

Now, what do you want to do before you begin? Pray, of course! Talk to the Author. Thank Him for speaking to you through His Word. Tell Him you want to honor and respect it by handling it with integrity instead of distorting it to make it say what you want it to say. Tell Him you want to learn truth and be changed by it. Ask Him to help you handle it accurately.

When you finish praying, read the first chapter and color code every reference to *the Lord* and *Jonah* (including pronouns). Then I'll share with you what to do next.

Color coding is one means to a good end. You've carefully identified pronouns and assigned them to the right persons by coloring them the same color. You've seen "who's who." The next step is to find out everything the chapter tells you about the *who*s.

Asking the 5 W's and an H

Look at the color-coded references to *the Lord,* and on a sheet of paper or in your Jonah notebook, list everything you learn from marking *the Lord.* This list will help you answer the "5 W's and an H"— the most important questions you can ask when studying the Bible or anything else. The 5 W's and an H are who, what, when, where, why, and how.

When you make your list, you will discover the who, the what, the when, the why, the where, and the how straight from the Word of God

An experimental study by Lamberski and Dwyer revealed that color-coding techniques are great instructional strategies. They found that color coding improves attention, learner motivation, and structure in memory (www.ed.psu.edu/dwyer/ researchjustification.htm).

itself. And if you don't add anything to or subtract anything from the text, you'll find yourself discovering truth! God's words are true, and simply listing the facts will help you handle His Word accurately so you understand what God has *said* and what He *means*. Then, Beloved, you know that you know what you are to believe and how you are to behave. And this makes you more than a conqueror of every situation of life.

You can make your lists about *the Lord* and *Jonah* together or separately—whichever suits your learning style.

Now, let's see how this works. Jonah 1:1 mentions *the Lord* and *Jonah*. What do you learn about the Lord in this verse?

You learn that the Lord spoke to Jonah. This tells you *what* the Lord did, so you record this on your list. Now, what do you learn from marking *Jonah* in verse 1? You learn *who* he is—the son of Amitai. Although you don't know who Amitai is, this detail does identify Jonah. It has a purpose, so record it.

The Lord	Jonah
1:1 spoke to Jonah	1:1 is the son of Amitai
1:2 told Jonah to go to Nineveh and cry against it*	1:2 is told by the Lord to go to Nineveh and cry against it*
	1:3 rises up to go to Joppa to flee to Tarshish from the presence of the Lord

*You can put this information either place, but only one place is necessary.

When you finish listing what you see in the rest of chapter 1, don't put down your pen or pencil and walk away. You want to apply truth to your life. Therefore, take time to reflect on what you learned from marking and listing the references to *the Lord* and *Jonah. Reflect* means meditate—chew on it, mull it over in your mind.

What has God just taught you about Himself? Do you believe everything you listed about Him—what He said, did, wanted?

If you don't believe something, ask yourself, *Why not?* If you do, what does this knowledge mean to your relationship to Him?

What do you learn about Jonah and especially from his relationship to the Lord? Look at the things you listed about him. Have you ever behaved in a similar way? This is how you apply what you've learned.

see journal

Jonah and You

Begin today with prayer and then review the lists you made about *the Lord* and *Jonah.* Read Jonah 1 again. Weren't you excited at what you learned about God? He speaks to man, hurls a wind, creates a storm, increases it, and then stops it. And then He appoints a fish to swallow a man! Wow! Is anything too difficult for the Lord?

The Where and the When

As you observe the text, you see several geographical references—Nineveh, Joppa, Tarshish. Events in the Bible occur in specific times and places. The place answers the key observation question *where?* Therefore, when you come to a geographical location, mark it distinctly so that you'll recognize it as a *where* in future readings. You may want to double underline the words in green. When I mark my Bible this way, I use a fine-point MicroPen.

As you read the text you also notice references to time. Time answers the question *when?* Days, months, years, and words like *before, after, then,* and *until* and other time references are very important because they put you into the historical context. Many times they help you interpret the text accurately—especially the prophetic passages. So learn to mark references to time distinctively. Many who study with us across the United States and around the world use a green circle or clock like this ⏱. Design and use whatever suits you.

- Now, mark geographical locations and time expressions in Jonah 1 on the observation worksheet on page 149–151.

- You can use the map below to see for yourself where these places are.

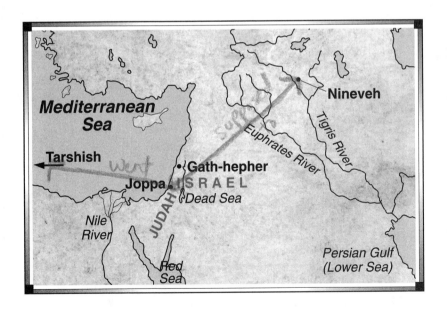

Did you notice where God wants Jonah and where Jonah goes? (Our children's Discover 4 Yourself inductive study on Jonah is titled *Wrong Way, Jonah!* You can understand why!) Contrast where Jonah starts out at the beginning of the chapter and where he is at the end. What does this tell you? Think about it—how would you apply this? Think about *how* he got there and *why* and *how long* Jonah was there.

Do you identify with Jonah in any way? Have you thought, *What a bull-headed man!*

You may want to jot down at least three insights on Jonah in the space following or in your notebook.

Finally, what is your prayer to God in the light of what you have observed? God has spoken to you in His Word. Do you have anything to say to Him in return? Recording the essence of your prayer can be helpful. Someday you may want to look at it and record what happened afterward. You can write your prayer in your notebook or below.

see journal

Thank you, Beloved, for honoring God by honoring His Word. For desiring and pursuing truth—the knowledge of God. For realizing that your body is His temple. For disciplining yourself so the Word of God dwells in you richly. May you prosper spiritually—exceedingly abundantly—beyond your wildest dreams!

Day Eleven

Context

Today we're going to take another look at the first chapter of Jonah because we have more to discover! So read through Jonah 1 again. This time mark the other characters in this chapter—the captain of the ship and the sailors. Once again, choose individual colors or color combinations. For example, you can color both the sailors and the captain orange, but underline captain with another color such as blue.

Make sure you color the respective pronouns. When you finish, look at each place you marked and list everything you learn about these men. Once again, this will help you discover the 5 W's and an H about these men. You can list your observations below, on a piece of paper, or in your Jonah notebook.

Context: What Is It and How Important Is It?

Now, let's pause and think through what you've learned up to this point. Observing all you can about people, places, and times helps you discern historical and geographical contexts.

Observing the context is an absolutely critical step to accurately interpreting Scripture. The Latin root *con* means "with," so *context* means "with (the) text." Context is the critical setting that rules all interpretation. We must never take God's words out of their context. If we do, then we'll have a pretext—something false that conceals the truth.

Among other things, context determines meanings of individual words that have multiple definitions. For example, *the trunk* in the sentence "When I heard the noise and saw the trunk up in the air, I became concerned" can belong to a car or to an elephant. The context will determine the meaning, so I have to read the sentences before and after this one.

As you observe and mark the text, you're learning the context in which something is being presented. This helps you determine what the text means so you can interpret it accurately. For instance, look at what you learn about...

- Nineveh (verse 2) *it's a great city*
- Joppa (verse 3) *it's down from where J is and it's a port for ships*
- direction of Tarshish in respect to Nineveh *away*
- modes of transportation (verse 3) *ship*
- the sailors
  - —their worship (verse 5) *to their own gods*
  - —power they ascribe to other gods (verse 6) *they think their god will help*
  - —connections they make between actions and calamities (verses 7-8) *Karma - if you did wrong it will show*

—how they learn things they don't know (verse 7) *Cast lots*

—their respect for gods (verse 10) *nothing compared to the true God*

—their take on killing innocent people (verse 14)
again dharma — if they kill, they will be killed

This simple exercise gives you insight into geographical, cultural, and spiritual settings in Jonah's day.

Day Twelve

Key Words

As you read a text of Scripture over and over and start marking people, places, and times, you're going to begin to discern what a particular chapter is about. Even if it doesn't mention specific people, it might mention different subjects. A book or a chapter or a segment of a book might be about people, events, teachings, prophecies, or wise sayings. It depends on the type of literature.

Key Words and Phrases

Now let's talk about key words. A key word is a word that is usually repeated in the text. Because it's repeated, it is important. Key words help you unlock the meaning of the text. They help you understand what the text is about—the main subjects in that text.

The Bible is an "oral" book. For millennia, until the invention of the printing press in the 1400s, it was heard more than it was read. The Scriptures were copied by hand and therefore were very scarce. People couldn't just pick up a Bible and read it as they do today.

Remember what you saw in 2 Kings 23:1-3? Josiah *read* the book of the Law to the people as they stood before the house of the Lord (the temple in Jerusalem). After the Babylonian captivity and the destruction of the temple, Israelites went to local synagogues to *hear* the Scriptures read. This is supported again when you read Revelation 1 and find a promise of blessing to those who read the words of prophecy and to those who hear.

Repetition is one of the essential components of learning. Therefore you will find key words (words important to understanding the text or getting the meaning across) repeated either throughout a book or in a segment or segments of that book.

Sometimes a key word is used profusely, as in 1 John 4, where *love* occurs 28 times in 21 verses. Other key words might be used much less, such as *walk,* which is used only 6 times in Ephesians 4–5. Yet the believer's walk with God is clearly what these two chapters are about. Whether 28 or 6 times, you know both words are key words because they unlock the meanings of their texts.

> *Thou shalt understand, therefore, that the Scripture hath but one sense, which is the literal sense. And that literal sense is the root and ground of all, and the anchor that never faileth, whereunto if thou cleave thou canst never err nor go out of the way. And if thou leave the literal sense, thou canst not but go out of the way.*
>
> WILLIAM TYNDALE

Sometimes a word or phrase actually shows the segments or portions of a book. For example, in Matthew you find the phrase "When Jesus had finished these sayings" (or something similar) five times between chapters 7 and 26. Each time the phrase is used it concludes a teaching segment. From 1 Corinthians 7 forward you find the phrase "Now concerning…" as Paul moves from issue to issue existing in the church at Corinth.

As you observe texts over and over (as you did with Jonah) and list your insights, key words begin to surface and provide a greater understanding of what God is saying—the points He wants to get across.

Jonah 1 includes several key words and phrases. Maybe you've noticed them already.

When you find a key word or phrase, mark it in a distinctive way using color(s) and/or symbols of your choice. This will help you readily see where they are used and how often.

You might also consider, especially when studying a longer book of the Bible, making what we call a "key word bookmark." On a 3 x 5 card, record the key words and phrases you want to mark in a book. Color code them on the bookmark as you will mark them in the Bible. The *NISB (New Inductive Study Bible)* gives you the major key words for most of the books of the Bible.

Let me give you an example. One key word in Jonah is *calamity*. It's an important word that I mark throughout my Bible because I want to know what the Word of God says about calamity. So whenever I come across *calamity* I put a black cloud around it like this and color it red.

Once I've marked a key word, I examine its context (setting) to see what I can learn about it. I want to see how it's used and what's said about it.

- Read Jonah 1 again. Mark *calamity* and list your insights.

see journal

- Now read through chapter 1 and find other key words and phrases that occur in these first 17 verses. List them below and add what you learn about them.

Day Thirteen

Listing Your Observations

If you're like me, you want to make sure you're getting it—you're learning what you ought to learn. So let's stop and look at what you observed yesterday in Jonah chapter 1.

One of the first key phrases you may have marked is *from the presence of the LORD.* It's used two times in verse 3—practically on top of each other—which looks like God doesn't want you to miss it. Then it's repeated again in verse 10. Now ask yourself what it means. And consider this: If God is omnipresent (everywhere) and omniscient (all knowing), how can anyone literally run away from God's presence?

If running from God's physical presence doesn't make sense, what does? Well, look at the context. God tells Jonah to go one direction, and Jonah goes another. Wrong way, Jonah!

Jonah knows exactly what he's doing. Look at verses 9-10. After he tells the sailors he's a Hebrew and that he fears the Lord God of heaven who made the sea and the dry land, the sailors become frightened and ask how he can be doing what he's doing.

And what is Jonah doing? The text says the men "knew that he was fleeing from the presence of the LORD, because he had told them."

So how would you interpret *fleeing from the presence of the Lord* in light of this context? Is it physical or moral—hiding or disobedience?

If you read on, you'll discover that Jonah knows God knows where he is: "For I know that on account of me this great storm has come upon you." Fleeing from the presence of the Lord was walking away from the will of the Lord. Living away from God's presence, then, means living in rebellion. When we obey, we move toward God.

Speaking of storms, did you mark the references to *storm on the sea?* Maybe you marked just *wind, storm,* and *sea.* The techniques you chose doesn't matter—the purpose is to observe the text carefully so you don't miss a thing. Look at verses 4, 11-12, and 13. What do these have to do with calamity? Any connection?

What kind of calamity struck them? A storm! And where did it come from? How did it happen? Who hurled the great wind on the sea? Watch the progression—the winds increase, the sea rages, and it doesn't stop raging until it gets Jonah!

God is behind the calamity. The Lord God of heaven who made the sea and the dry land stirred up the storm and stopped the storm—all to accomplish His purpose. And the same God who made the sea appointed a fish to swallow Jonah.

Interesting, isn't it? Now what can you say to people who don't want to believe that these events were sovereign acts of God? What can you *show* them?

You can show them just what you studied and discovered for yourself. First, Jonah obviously believed God was in control (1:12); so did the sailors (1:14-16). If people today don't believe, the facts don't change...and everyone is responsible to believe them. Our beliefs don't manufacture facts, and their disbelief can't make them go away; neither ever alters truth, and you and I need to remember that. The Bible is God's Word, and God doesn't lie.

When you marked Jonah 1, did you notice references to *prayer?* Whenever you study the Bible, may I suggest you mark references to prayer so you can learn what the Word of God says about this vital subject. Of course you also want to mark synonyms for *prayer* (like *call* and *cry*) the same way. Read chapter 1 now and mark any references to *prayer.* Write down any insights you might glean on prayer from this chapter.

Finally, as you made your list about the sailors, didn't you love watching what happened as they went through this experience? Has anything happened in your life these past 13 days as a result of doing this study? Write your experiences out below and then bring today's study to a close by taking time to talk to the Lord God of heaven who made the sea and the dry land.

see journal

By the way, Beloved, did you notice how many times you read the text of Jonah 1—maybe five or six times. Reading and marking are excellent ways to hide God's Word in your heart so that He can bring the truth to your remembrance at any place or time or in any situation and so you can live in a manner pleasing to Him.

The Best Interpreter
of Scripture

God's *entire* Word is truth, and He never contradicts Himself. Rather, God explains truth with truth. This is why studying the Bible book by book and continuously reading through it is so helpful. In doing so, you are learning the whole counsel of God.

The Best Interpreter of Scripture Is Scripture

Scripture is the most valuable commentary on Scripture. As you read and mark texts, you find the Spirit of God reminding you of similar scriptures that clarify and explain them. When this happens, you want to write down these "cross-references." Many Bibles have textual footnotes and cross-references in margins beside the verses. These are usually good and helpful, but nothing beats writing down your own!

When I read Jonah 1:14 for instance, I saw the concern of the sailors expressed in their prayer: "We earnestly pray, O Lord, do not let us perish on account of this man's life and do not put innocent blood on us; for You, O Lord have done as You have pleased." I realized they understood the sanctity of life and their accountability before God. My mind immediately went to Genesis 9:5-6, so I went there, verified the reference, and wrote it in my Bible next to Jonah 1:14. Here's what it says:

> Surely I will require your lifeblood; from every beast I will require it. And from every man, from every man's brother I will require the life of man. Whoever sheds man's blood, by man his blood shall be shed, for in the image of God He made man.

Next to Genesis 9:5-6, I also wrote a list of other scriptures related to the same subject—a *topical list* on the subject presented in Genesis 9:5-6. I usually do this in pencil so I can erase and reorder or rework my list. By the way, this is how you can build your knowledge of God.

When I came to Jonah 1:17, I wrote Matthew 12:38-40 and 16:4 next to it because it states Jonah was in the stomach of the great fish three days and three nights. The time phrase and reference to Jonah reminded me of these two passages:

> Then some of the scribes and Pharisees said to Him, "Teacher, we want to see a sign from You." But He answered and said to them, "An evil and adulterous generation craves for a sign; and *yet* no sign will be given to it but the sign of Jonah the prophet; for just as Jonah was three days and three nights in the belly of the sea monster, so will the Son of Man be three days and three nights in the heart of the earth.

> "An evil and adulterous generation seeks after a sign; and a sign will not be given it, except the sign of Jonah." And He left them and went away.

Many people may call Jonah's story a myth, but Jesus didn't. The three days and three nights Jonah spent in the stomach of a fish wasn't simply a whale of a tale! Jesus the Son of God, the Way, the Truth, and the Life, compared Jonah's incarceration to His own death and resurrection. Think about what the sovereign God did about 775 years before His Son's death—the magnitude of the sign He gave us. Then think about how you know this. You know it by comparing Scripture with Scripture.

Get in the habit of recording significant cross-references in your Bible or highlighting them in some way if you have marginal references in your study Bible that give additional insight into what you just read in the text. We are going to talk about cross-referencing Scripture with Scripture in greater depth later, so this is enough for right now. However, let me remind you of a very important truth when studying your Bible: Scripture will never contradict Scripture. It can't. All Scripture, whether the book of Genesis or Matthew or Revelation, comes from the same source—the mouth of God. The Bible was not devised by man—it is "God-breathed"!

Now, Beloved, as we bring this week to a close, stop and think about all you learned from this first chapter of Jonah. We live with so much noise and busyness that we often don't take enough time to be quiet and think about truth, life, where we are headed, where we want to go, and what we want to accomplish.

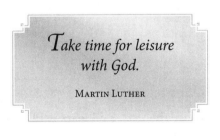

Take time for leisure with God.

MARTIN LUTHER

Consequently we move randomly and purposelessly through life. Pretty soon the years have passed, and we're no different.

We've grown older but not wiser—we haven't matured into the stature of the fullness of Christ as Ephesians 4:13-16 says we should. We look at others and feel light-years behind—all because we didn't *bask* in the light of His Word.

Thinking and actively listening; not adding to the text what we imagine would happen, but with great reverence, carefully and accurately observing what God has said, picturing it, meditating on it—this is what will make the difference in your character and in the way you spend your remaining days on earth. As you study your Bible, allow time to absorb truth—to think about how it can instruct you, encourage you, and give you wisdom, understanding, counsel, and hope.

Take a moment, Beloved, as we bring this day to a close, to jot down insights you want to remember. Then turn what you learned into prayer—which will help you remember even more! You can do this here or in your Jonah notebook.

love and forgiveness. how to move forward.

By the way, my heart is filled with such affection for you. Thank you for wanting to know God, to understand Him, and to love Him with all your heart, soul, mind, body, and strength. I am so honored that you would read this book.

WEEK THREE

Turning to God

What do you do when you find yourself in trouble and distressed? Do you freeze, feeling paralyzed with no way out? Then what do you do? Wallow in your woe? Medicate your sorrows with food, alcohol, drugs, or distracting entertainment like television, a buying spree, an affair, or the Internet's chat rooms and pornography? Or do you simply sleep?

Or do you seek help, and if you do, where do you turn? Let's see what we can learn from Jonah.

Jonah found himself in a most unusual situation. Rather confining, don't you think? Shut off from everyone...everyone but One, that is!

As you begin in prayer,

> *Alexander Hamilton (delegate to the U.S. Constitutional Convention, principal author of the Federalist Papers, and the first and most influential Secretary of the Treasury) read everything out loud. It helped him become an attorney in nine months. He believed it helped his speaking and expression. Thomas Jefferson wrote the Declaration of Independence, but Hamilton's oratory helped convince the others to sign it.*

let me share Psalm 119:169: "Let my cry come before You, O LORD; give me understanding according to Your word."

Now take a look at the last verse of Jonah 1 and from there read all of chapter 2. May I suggest you read the text out loud. Saying and hearing it at the same time will help you remember the words of God.

- Now read Jonah 2 again and color code references to *the Lord* and to *Jonah* as you did when you studied chapter 1.

- As you do, make sure you mark everything that answers *where?* Remember, you want to mark *all* geographical references. Double underline these in green.

- Mark everything that answers *when?* Use a clock or whatever you chose to mark references to time or sequence of time, such as *then* in 2:1.

- After you mark the references to Jonah, list what you observed about him—the __ W's and an __ (fill in the blanks) concerning Jonah. Don't miss where Jonah is when the chapter opens and when it closes.

- Now list what you observed about God from this chapter. Don't miss a thing!

You began today's study with prayer, crying to God for understanding. How would you close it in prayer? Write out your prayer to the God you've just observed.

Day Sixteen

What Can I Learn About Prayer?

The two weakest disciplines in the lives of many people who profess to know God, young and old, are Bible study and prayer. The crises of life often drive us to both. We become desperate. We realize no one can help us but God, and then we cry out. We want answers we can trust, so we decide we want to know what God says.

Haven't you seen this in individuals? In nations, during times of national crisis?

After terrorists launched attacks on the World Trade Center's twin towers in New York City and also on the Pentagon and White House on 9/11/2001, churches were packed. People wanted to know if this was the beginning of the end. Was Armageddon coming? What does the Bible say?

But later, unfortunately, the question lost relevance, and church attendance for the most part returned to previous numbers. The enemy hadn't invaded our shores again, so the pressure was off.

As you saw yesterday, when Jonah was in grave circumstances, "Jonah prayed to the Lord from the stomach of the fish."

Read through Jonah 2 again. Remember how you marked references to *prayer* in chapter 1? Now do the same in Jonah 2, including synonyms like *cry*.

When you finish marking the text, list below what you learned about prayer. See if the text tells you what caused Jonah to pray.

in journal

Now, just so you and I make sure we don't miss anything, I want to give you some questions to answer. Asking questions is a good way to make sure we don't miss relevant information. As you answer these, record the verses you find your answers in:

1. According to Jonah 2:2 where was Jonah when he cried out?

   Welly of a fish
   depth of see

2. What was Jonah's assessment of his condition, and why did he think he was in this predicament?

   V8 he regarded a vain idol
   V4 he lost sight of God / holy temple

3. You know from chapter 1 that Jonah willfully disobeyed

God. In light of this, did Jonah have the right to pray? Many people assume that once they willfully disobey God, prayer won't work. So why even bother? But is this true? Can we learn anything from the text? (The answer lies in Jonah's words.)

he looked to God and (v 9) vowed to do something and would pay that vow

4. What did God do? What does this tell you about Him? What can you learn from this for your life?

V10 he Commanded the fish and Jonah came out of whale

- He forgives, He listens, He's giving another chance

5. Finally, have you ever chosen not to pray because you thought it wouldn't do any good? Why did you think that way? Have you learned anything today that would challenge this thinking?

yes, I have thought that. I thought that way because I had deliberately sinned but I see in Jonah's case that God forgave him and gave him a chance to try again

Well, Beloved, this is enough to contemplate today. Remember to take what you learned to the Lord. Talk with Him about it.

Chapter Themes and At a Glance Charts

Creating an accurate summary of something helps you to grasp it and process what you heard or studied. This is what we want to do today with the content of the first two chapters of Jonah.

When you finish observing a chapter of Scripture, make a habit of summarizing the content of the chapter in as few words as possible.

Chapter Themes

How do you summarize the first two chapters of Jonah—or any chapter in the Bible? First, discern what is the chapter's main event or subject. What is talked about the most? We call this the theme.

Once you see this, summarize it in as few words as possible. Use significant words from the chapter for themes (titles)—key words are especially good. Be as concise as possible, make your summary memorable, and stick to the text.

Now, let's consider Jonah 1–2. Write the themes below.

Jonah 1—

Jonah 2—

Now ask yourself if your themes capture what the chapters are about. The themes should distinguish one chapter from another. Do they? Polish the themes if necessary.

At a Glance Charts

Record the themes in pencil on the "Jonah at a Glance" chart on page 102. Do this for Jonah 1 and 2.

Record these themes as you move through the book chapter by chapter. When you finish the book, review your "At a Glance" chart. If you are satisfied with the chapter themes, record them in ink.

Summarizing the text and recording it on the "At a Glance" chart is a very valuable process in Bible study. It helps you crystallize and remember what you've learned and see how the book fits together chapter by chapter and segment by segment. It also creates a great reference tool for longer books, helping you readily locate major events and truths.

When you complete the "At a Glance" chart, you'll have formulated your own outline of the book that you studied for yourself. If you have an *NISB (New Inductive Study Bible)* and record your insights in it on the "At a Glance" charts at the end of every book of the Bible, you'll always have those outlines with you for ready reference.

Now, Beloved, as we bring this day and the second chapter

of Jonah to a close, ask yourself if you really believe what you just studied. I mean *really* believe. Believing is our first step in application; don't ever downplay it, Beloved. According to 2 Timothy 3:16-17, Scripture is profitable for doctrine— for teaching. You've been taught. You've learned. But do you believe?

Do you believe it so much that you'd tell a room full of people you know about a man who thought he could run away from God but ended up in the stomach of a great fish, where he spent three days and three nights until God made the fish vomit him up on shore?

What would you do, my friend, if they laughed at you and called you a fool? How would you answer? How secure would you be in your answer?

By the way, did you know the whole book of Jonah is in the Koran, the Muslims' holy book? What might happen if you were to pray and then, if God leads, invite some Muslims to your home to do this study with you? Or is the idea of associating with them repulsive because you just don't like them or what they believe?

If the answer is yes, *Ohhhhh, Jonah!*

Hello, Nineveh!

Today we come to the third chapter of Jonah—another short chapter of just ten verses, and yet much happens. What's the first thing you want to do (*after* prayer), student of the Bible, if you want to discover the truths of this chapter for yourself? Write out your answer.

If you answered anything about observing the text, you're on course, and I'm proud of you! We've talked about it, you've done it, and you've remembered. Now, keep on doing it, my friend.

- Mark the people and words you marked before (the ones you listed on your key word bookmark if you made one), time phrases, and geographical references.

- List what you learn about *the Lord* and about *Jonah* on the chart below.

The Lord	Jonah

- Are there any other *whos* (important [key] people) you need to pay attention to? If so, list them.

- Did you see new key words or phrases? List them below. If you are using a bookmark, record them.

This has been a good day's worth of study, a good beginning. As you observed the text, did you see anything that especially caught your attention? Anything about God? About Jonah? Any truths that encourage you? Write them out, and we'll come back to the chapter tomorrow.

Day Nineteen

When Do You Go Outside the Bible?

Remember, Beloved, the key to understanding the Bible is *observe, observe, observe!* The more you see what the text says, the easier it will be to understand.

God told Jonah to go to Nineveh and cry against it (1:2), so you will want to learn everything you can about the city. As you'll see, a city is not just bricks and mortar; it's people, it's leadership. Therefore, mark all references to *Nineveh* and ask the 5 W's and an H so you can discover everything God wants you to know about it.

- You've double underlined *Nineveh* because it's a geographical location, but now you need to pick a color for it because it's the *most important location* in the book of Jonah. Mark every reference to *Nineveh*, including pronouns, in chapters 1, 2, and 3.

- Now list everything you learned about *Nineveh*. As you do this, let me say that as you study this way more and more, you'll find your observation skills becoming so much more acute, you won't have to make lists of everything you mark. By marking my Bible this way, I'm able to simply look at a text and review in my mind what I learn from the markings. But for now it's good practice to write out your list.

see journal

- In the process of observing the text and making your lists, did you notice key words or phrases? Once again, until you develop an observing eye, you'll usually pick up the key words and phrases when you make your lists. Now, what new key words did you see in chapter 3? List them below.

word of the Lord

sack cloth

relent

great city

- I don't know if you wrote it down, but *the word of the Lord* is mentioned three times in this chapter. I have chosen to mark every reference to *the word of the Lord* when I read my Bible. I draw a symbol like this 📖 over it with my purple MicroPen, and then I color it green.

- You'll find *the word of the Lord* also in Jonah 1:1. Review Jonah 1:1 and compare it with Jonah 3. What do you observe?

  *It stopped w/ Jonah's sin in chapter.
  in chapter 3 it is able to continue
  on and do good work*

- I always mark references to *fasting* in my Bible. I want to learn all I can about this spiritual discipline. I color the word (and its synonyms and pronouns) purple and underline it in brown. *Fasting* is referred to twice in this chapter. Once it's just used; the other time it's described. Mark *fasting* in Jonah 3. What did you learn? As you list insights, don't miss the who, why, how, and what. Who fasted? Why did they fast? How (to what degree)? How long? What was the result?

  *the ppl fasted and cried out to God. They
  didn't eat or drink. It was from king
  to pauper. even animals couldn't eat or drink—
  was this so that no one would have to work
  while fasting?*

- As you listed what you learned about *Nineveh,* including its people, you probably saw *sackcloth* repeated. I marked it with a black half circle like this ⌒ and colored the inside purple. What did you learn from marking it? List your insights below.

  that when the people started fasting and repented they covered themselves w/ it

Now beloved, once you finish your observations, review them. Then investigate things you don't understand—search for their meanings. For instance, if you want to learn more about fasting or sackcloth, go to your study tools and see what you learn from the definition of the words and their uses in other places in the Bible. When you finish exploring what you can observe from the Word, go to outside helps such as Bible dictionaries and commentaries.

We can't highlight this enough: Always thoroughly search the Word first and then consider the (hopefully scholarly) opinions of men. If you follow this pattern, you'll be able to differentiate good from bad opinions. Your personal inductive study of the Bible is your plumb line for checking everything.

Concordances

One of the most useful tools in Bible study is a concordance. A concordance alphabetically lists every word used in the Bible (from the English translation) along with all the places where that word is found in both the Old Testament and the New Testament. It also gives a brief definition of the word, along with the Hebrew, Aramaic, or Greek word.

Concordances are available as computer programs as well as books. If you have a computer, we highly recommend you get a good Bible study program, or you can check a concordance or other word study tools online. For instance, links to many study tools are available at www.preceptaustin.org. Or for more written information on Bible study helps and how they work, see my book *How to Study the Bible,* published by Harvest House Publishers.

Concordances and Cross-References

One of the things you might check in the concordance is the list of references to Jonah. You'll find Jonah mentioned in 2 Kings 14:25; Matthew 12:39-41; 16:4; and Luke 11:29-30,32. We looked at Jesus' references to Jonah already; however, you could look up the one in 2 Kings and see if it refers to the same Jonah. This is where his genealogy, which you marked in Jonah 1, is helpful.

The concordance is a valuable tool for cross-referencing. When you look up corresponding words in other portions of the Bible, you often gain further insight into various topics in the text. For example, when studying Jonah 3, you might also want to look up other references to *fasting* and *sackcloth* and learn what the Bible teaches on the subjects.

Application

Finally, Beloved, give yourself time to reflect on what you learn and apply it to your life. Ask yourself why God put what you just studied in His book and told you to study it. Handle the Word accurately, cutting it straight like the workman who is never ashamed (2 Timothy 2:15).

For example, after you've read Jonah 3, you can ask yourself these questions:

- How many times has God spoken to me about something I need to do, some issue I need to resolve?

- How long do I take to obey? Why? What is true if I don't obey at all?

- What soul-searching situations has God placed me in? How serious should I be about fasting? Why don't I fast more?

As you sit and think, faithful one, ask God to speak to you, to search your heart. Application will come—if not now, then later. Rest assured—it will come.

Day Twenty

On Your Own

Are you excited about what you're learning? I am! I'm thrilled that you and I have reached this point. You've learned so much, and the journey isn't over! After we finish Jonah, I'm going to take you to the New Testament. Studying different kinds of passages will help you get a solid start in this new life-transforming adventure of inductive study.

I led you through the process of observing the first three chapters of Jonah. Now it's your turn. Use what you've learned to observe Jonah 4. Look for new key words to mark. If you see any, list them below.

Day Twenty-One

Contrasts and Comparisons

Here we go—our last day of study in the book of Jonah! Were you surprised by the abrupt ending of Jonah? It makes us wonder what point God wants to leave us with.

As you studied Jonah, you created profiles of God and Jonah. What did you learn about God from this book? What struck your heart? What insights about God will you take away? Will they impact the way you live? If so, how? Take a few minutes to write out your thoughts.

Now, let's talk about God. *Appointed* is used three times in this chapter and once in Jonah 1:17. This makes it important, especially since God is the One who appoints. Note *what* God appoints and *why*. Then think about what this tells you about Him. Record your insights.

> God appointed a plant to give Jonah shade
> God appointed a worm to take away the shade
> God appointed even more hardship by bringing
> scorching east wind
>
> It shows God gives and takes away

Did you notice *compassion* and *compassionate* repeated? If not, read the chapter again and mark the references. What did you learn from marking these words?

> Jonah knew God was compassionate
> God had compassion on the city of Nineveh
> Jonah had compassion for a plant

Discover the Truth About God

If you want to know truth about God, you'll find it in His Word because this is where God reveals Himself. Therefore whenever you study the Bible, make sure you learn everything

He reveals about Himself through His actions, His judgments, and His statements about His character.

If you're familiar with the first five books of the Bible (the Torah), you probably recognized Jonah's description of God in Jonah 4:2. It's taken from Exodus 34:5-7, an ancient description of God that everyone needs to know and remember.[1] The question, however, is, how do you find these corresponding verses?

Since *compassion* is a key word used to describe God, you may want to see where else this word is used. How? A word search in a concordance would lead you to Exodus 34:5-7 and other verses.

- Read Exodus 34:5-7. Note God's description, who describes Him this way, and how this description compares with Jonah's statement about Him.

- When you saw Jonah's description of God as One who relents, did you remember this was not the first use of *relent?* Read Jonah 3:9-10. Mark *relent.* I did it with an arrow like this. ↵ Now, what did you learn from marking *relent?*

- What does Jonah's statement about God in 4:2 tell you about Jonah—what's he aware of?

---

1. I recommend writing it somewhere in the front of your Bible for quick reference.

- God brings the book to a close with a reference to His *compassion.* How does this key word help you understand the book of Jonah?

- Did you notice Jonah had compassion? What was the object of Jonah's compassion?

- By the way, did you mark *anger* and *angry?* They are important words (also look at Jonah 3:9). What do you learn from marking these key words?

- According to the book of Jonah, why was God angry with Nineveh?

- Why was Jonah angry?

Contrast and Comparisons

I hope you're enjoying the process of acquiring some new tools for studying God's Word. Here's another important one. As you observe Scripture, watch for comparisons and contrasts.

By pointing out similarities, *comparisons* illumine, illustrate, and strengthen authors' points. They often include words like *like* and *as*.

Contrasts show differences within the text. Sometimes, *but* signifies a contrast. Let me give you two examples.

- Proverbs 13:20 shows a contrast between the companions of a wise man and of a fool. "He who walks with wise men will be wise, but the companion of fools will suffer harm."

- First Thessalonians 5:4-10 contrasts the behavior of the sons of darkness with that of the sons of light. It also contrasts the day and the night.

What contrast do you see in Jonah 4, and what point does this contrast make?

Jonah wanted to die. Have you ever wanted to die? I have! Why? Because life wasn't the way I wanted—I was under pressure and hurting badly. As I think about it, wanting to die was my way of putting myself in place of God. I wanted out because the sovereign God was allowing something that wasn't pleasing to me. Have you ever been there? If you have, why did *you* want out?

- Did you mark references to *death?* I usually draw a black tombstone like this ⌂ over *death, dying, killed, perished*—any word that pertains to cessation of life. Look at the references to *death* and *perishing* in Jonah. If you didn't mark them, do so.

- What did you learn about Jonah from marking these references?

Did you notice the questions God asked Jonah? Think about how you can apply these questions to your life. For example, when you get angry, think of your Father asking *you,* "Do you have good reason to be angry?" (4:4). List some things you have been tempted to be angry about.

- Now, stop for a few minutes and review what you marked about Jonah in this fourth chapter. Think again of the contrast between God and Jonah. Who are you more like? Do you need to make any changes, Beloved? Be specific in your responses to these questions.

- What point does God make at the close of this book?

Pause for a moment and ask yourself, *Do I have more compassion for things that make me comfortable than for people who make me uncomfortable?* Did you see the contrast—things or people?

Well, Beloved, we've come to the end of our study on Jonah. You've seen far more than we've discussed because you learned to discover truth for yourself. I'd love to hear about all you've seen—what God has taught you. I love knowing we can say with the psalmist, "You Yourself have taught me" (Psalm 119:102).

JONAH AT A GLANCE

Theme of Jonah:

	SEGMENT DIVISIONS		CHAPTER THEMES
Author:			
			1
Date:			
Purpose:			
			2
Key Words:			
Jonah			
compassion (compassionate)			
relent(s)			3
turn (turned)			
pray (any reference to prayer or calling out to God)			
perish (death)			
Lord (God)			4
appointed			
anger (angry)			
calamity (and synonyms)			

WEEK FOUR

The Author, His Purpose, and the Recipients

Welcome to the New Testament! We're going to study the book of Jude. I chose this book because it's short—very doable in the time we have left. Take some time to prepare your heart in prayer.

I'd like you to begin by simply reading Jude so you can get an overview. Stop and do that now. You'll find it on pages 143–145.

Now remember, when you study a book of the Bible, your first step is observation—seeing what the text says. And what do you begin with? Remember? With the easiest things to see—people! The *who!*

Jude is an epistle (a letter). When you study an epistle (most of the books in the New Testament are epistles), see what you can learn about the person who wrote it and the individual or people to whom the letter was written—the recipient or recipients. These people are the easiest to observe.

Many times (but not always) the writer identifies himself with personal pronouns like *I, me,* and *my.* He may also use the plural pronouns *we* and *us.*

Recipients are most often designated *you* and *your* and

sometimes collectively as *brethren, beloved,* or in James, *beloved brethren.* When I call you "Beloved," you're hearing not only the sentiment of my heart speaking but also God's Word to you! He loves you first and most and gives me a love for you as brothers and sisters in Christ. And I'm in good company with many New Testament writers.

An Overview and the Author's Purpose

As you read Jude or any other New Testament book, look for the author's purpose for writing. I get an overview of a book before I study it chapter by chapter. This helps me keep things in the context of the big picture. The overview gives me the author's purpose. Sometimes authors state their purposes. When they don't, however, you can extract it from the content of the book. The author's content will reveal his purpose. You'll see it in such things as repetition, emphasis, instructions, admonitions, warnings, and appeals.

Now then, after you take a few moments to pray, begin by reading through Jude. Color code references to the author one color and references to the recipient(s) another. I use the same colors throughout my Bible—authors blue, recipients orange. Be sure to mark their pronouns and synonyms. When you finish, list everything you learn about each.

Author	Recipients

We're going to delve into what Jude says *to* and *about* the recipients because we can learn much for our lives, but we'll do this later, so hangeth thou in there!

- Does the author state his reason for writing? If so, write it out and record the verse where you found it.

- What are your impressions of this book after today's study?

That's it for today, Beloved. You're off to a good start. Thank you for studying to show yourself approved unto Him. How I pray you'll urge others to do the same. Think of what would happen in the church of Jesus Christ if we all disciplined ourselves to be godly. Jesus prayed for all believers, "Father, sanctify them in the truth; Your word is truth" (John 17:17).

Day Twenty-Three

Getting an Overview

Jude, the brother of Jesus Christ, wrote to urge believers to earnestly contend for the faith that was once for all handed down to the saints. (Once for all!—interesting phrase isn't it?)

Contend for the faith! Did you see *why?* Because "certain persons have crept in unnoticed...ungodly persons" (verse 4). Here's another *who* you need to pay attention to.

What does Jude tell us about these ungodly persons? If they crept in unnoticed, can we identify them? Are these ungodly people in the church today mingling with Christians and calling themselves Christians?

Our next task is to see if we can answer these questions from the text.

- Now faithful one, read through Jude and color every reference to *ungodly persons,* including synonyms and pronouns.

- You marked every reference to the *ungodly.* Now list what you saw about ungodly persons under the heading on the next page. As I said earlier, making lists will help you train your eye to see everything there is to see when you mark a word or a phrase. Listing is another way to let the Holy Spirit seal God's truths in your mind so He can bring them to your remembrance when you need them.

What Jude Teaches About Ungodly Persons

Now, for the sake of clarity, let's stop and get the big picture of Jude. After you
read an epistle,
do an overview,
see who wrote it,
note to whom it was written,
and discover the basic content of each chapter,
it's good to stop and reflect on the letter as a whole. So let's do that now that we've observed the major *who*s: the author, the recipients, and the ungodly. Answer the following questions:

- What is Jude writing about? (Was this what he intended to write about?)

- Why is he writing about this subject? His *reason* for writing determines *what* he writes about.

- What does Jude emphasize in his letter?

- How does he lay out his letter? Since Jude is only one chapter long, we'll look at it paragraph by paragraph. The New American Standard Bible indicates paragraph divisions with bold verse numbers. Read each paragraph, write out what it's about, and you'll be finished for the day. Be as brief as possible.

    verses 1-2—

    verses 3-4—

    verses 5-7—

    verses 8-13—

verses 14-16—

verses 17-23—

verses 24-25—

Well done! You may not understand all the details and probably have lots of questions, but doing this gives you a good general understanding of what this letter is all about, doesn't it? And that's important.

If you get caught up in details and lose the big picture, you're more likely to take things out of context. This is how Scripture gets distorted.

How well this was illustrated one night when I heard a very well-known TV personality teaching on our need for an "anointed leader" if we want to experience the power of God in our lives. He used Jeremiah 7:18 to prove his point as he drew attention to the fact that children could *gather* wood, but only fathers could *kindle* the fire. That was the only part of the verse he quoted.

The man documented his teaching with a verse taken out of context. In the passage, God is illustrating the sins of His people in Jerusalem:

> "The children gather wood, and the fathers kindle the fire, and the women knead dough to make cakes for the queen of heaven; and they pour

out drink offering to other gods in order to spite Me. Do they spite Me?" declares the LORD. "Is it not themselves they spite, to their own shame?" (Jeremiah 7:18-19).

Even if these were not *sinful* actions, God did not say children *can't* kindle fires. First of all, these are all descriptive, not imperative (oughts and ought nots). And secondly, none of them use "only." Yet those listening who did not know the Word of God and did not check out the verse believed this man's teaching. Oh, Beloved, do you see the importance of studying God's Word for ourselves so we aren't led astray by every wind of doctrine and cunning craftiness of men?

If you and I don't honor the Bible as God's Word and take the time and discipline we need to handle it accurately, we'll distort it to our own destruction (2 Peter 3:16). This, Beloved, is what inductive study is all about—giving the Bible the honor it deserves.

> *Study it carefully, think on it prayerfully. Deep in your heart, let its oracles dwell... Study its mystery, slight not its history. No man ere knew it or loved it too well.*
>
> AUTHOR UNKNOWN

Remember my illustration of peeling the onion—taking it apart layer by layer until you get to the core? Well, you've done some good peeling.

Be encouraged today by Jude 24-25 (good verses to memorize), which give us great assurance of our Father's keeping power. May you be kept, Beloved! Kept by Christ!

Day Twenty-Four

Know the Meaning of Words

Communication is all about words—about understanding what someone is saying. Therefore if you are going to understand God, you have to understand the meaning of the words He uses.

Know the Meaning of Words

Did you notice any words in Jude that were difficult to understand? Maybe they were words that you don't use every day. For instance—*licentiousness.* Licentiousness certainly describes our times, but do you know what *licentiousness* means?

If you're using a trustworthy translation of the Bible (rather than a paraphrase), you're pretty safe in checking out the English definition of a word in a dictionary because the translators tried to choose words closest to the biblical authors' intent. Thus a good translation that sticks as close as it can word for word puts you on pretty solid ground. The translations I think are closest to the author's intent include the New American Standard Bible (NASB), which is the translation I am using in this book, the King James Version (KJV), the New King James Version (NKJV), and the English Standard Version (ESV).

Now then, all that said, let's make sure we know what licentiousness is. If you know its meaning, record it. If you don't know its meaning, look it up in a dictionary and write out its definition.

Licentiousness is…

Now do you understand why I said licentiousness describes our times? People are living in moral anarchy!

Hebrew and Greek Word Studies

Sometimes you'll want to do word studies using tools that take you back to the original language to make sure you know exactly what's being said—how and why the author uses the words that he does to express himself.

The Old Testament was written in Hebrew—the language of Israel—and some Aramaic. Aramaic was the trade language of the times.

The New Testament was written exclusively in Koine Greek, the common but precise Greek spread by Alexander the Great as he set about conquering the world. Although the prophet Daniel prophesied about him, Alexander didn't live until intertestamental times. However, the Greek language he used in Hellenizing the kingdoms he conquered continued right through the days of Jesus and His apostles.

As I said, many times you can sharpen your understanding of a text by doing a word study on a particular word. If it is an Old Testament word, you would look up the Hebrew or

Aramaic equivalent by using the concordance, see how it is defined, and then possibly do a more in-depth study of the word and its use by consulting a word study book like the *Theological Wordbook of the Old Testament* (TWOT).

If it is a New Testament word, you would look up the Greek word in the concordance, see how it is defined, and then once again possibly turn to other excellent word study books available today.

All of this is explained in greater detail, and step-by-step, in my book *How to Study the Bible.*[2] Now then, that is enough for now about word studies.

Read through Jude again out loud. As you do, watch the flow of thought.

- Did you notice how Jude moves from the beloved to the ungodly and then back to the beloved? If not, read through the book again, noting where you marked the *beloved* and where you marked the *ungodly* and observe what is being said.

- How does Jude describe the ungodly in verse 4? What are they doing?

2. *How to Study the Bible* (Harvest House Publishers). It can be found at most Christian bookstores or ordered from Precept Ministries International either online from our website, www.precept.org, or by calling 1-800-763-1990.

- What is their destiny according to verse 4? Or to put it another way, what are they marked out for?

- Now watch how Jude supports their judgment. What does he do in verses 5-7?

Did you notice how Jude uses illustrations from Old Testament people and events to support the just condemnation of the ungodly who have crept into the church? I love watching the way Jude brings the Old into the New. The Old Testament is often used to support the New Testament—or to reveal in the New what was prophesied in the Old. Romans 15:4 tells us that "whatever was written in earlier times was written for our instruction, so that through perseverance and the encouragement of the Scriptures we might have hope."

When you review the references to the ungodly you'll see another key word—*condemnation*. You'll notice several synonyms for this as you work through the text.

- Read through Jude again and list the words used by Jude that have to do with *condemnation*.

- Decide how you want to mark these words and then mark them on your observation worksheet. I used a red pen and marked like this: W͡ .

- Now list below those who, according to Jude, suffer destruction, judgment, eternal fire, and black darkness—those who will perish.

Now then, as we wrap up today, let me give you the Greek equivalents of some of the words you just marked along with their definitions. I think these will help you appreciate the text even more.

- *condemnation* (verse 4): *krima*—to judge or condemn
- *destroyed* (verse 5, *perished* in verse 11): *apollumi*—to destroy utterly, not annihilate (end existence)
- *judgment* (verses 6 and 15): *krisis*—the act or process of judging
- *punishment* (verse 7): *dike*—execution of a sentence

As you bring today to a close, meditate on what you've seen in the Word of God. Chew these things over and over in your mind. Whether you're cleaning up after yourself, driving somewhere, doing some chore, or getting ready for bed, *think,* Beloved. You've been given the mind of Christ, so use your mind. Think about what you read, what you marked, what you learned.

In this case, think about why Jude is in the Word of God—what God wants you to know and do. Think beyond yourself. Think about how knowing the content of Jude can help you earnestly contend for the faith once for all delivered to the saints. You're a guardian of truth; how are you doing? What can you do? Ask, and your Master will answer. After all, this is kingdom business!

Day Twenty-Five

The Value of Asking Questions

Are you awed, Beloved, by what you're learning from Jude's letter to the called, the beloved in God the Father, who are kept for Jesus Christ? You should be! This is you if you are truly a child of God. You're hearing from God and discovering truth for yourself! And your education or lack thereof (that's me—no degrees!) isn't the issue. Rather, it is a matter of setting your heart on knowing God and disciplining yourself to achieve that goal. I'm so very proud of you.

Well, we have just four days left including today, so let's begin by praying together and then getting into Jude.

> *O Father, I thank You so very much for this dear child of Yours who so values Your Word and longs to know You more intimately and please You in every aspect of life.*
>
> *We come together in prayer, precious Lord, to ask You to use these final days of study to powerfully affect our lives. Thank You for speaking to us. May we understand and treasure Your words. Give us wisdom from above to know Your precepts for life,*

to live accordingly, and to valiantly contend for the faith You have handed down to us through Your inerrant, infallible Word. Build us up in our most holy faith. Remind us that grace is not license to live immorally but power to live righteously.

Father, I also ask You to lead this precious servant of Yours to teach others how to study Your Bible and handle it accurately. May we all find Your approval—as workmen who do not need to be ashamed.

I thank You, believing You'll answer this prayer because it's in accord with Your Word and will. We pray these things in the name above all names, the name of Your Son and our Savior, Jesus Christ, who lives to make intercession for us.

Amen and Amen.

Today we're going to see the marvelous way Jude highlights the condemnation of the ungodly using Old Testament illustrations.

Let's look at the first illustration Jude gives his readers in verse 5—the destruction of those who did not believe after God saved them from Egypt.

What do you do with this? You may not be familiar with what Jude is referring to (although his readers were. You can tell by Jude's words "remind you" and "though you know all things"). Therefore you would dig into God's Word to find out where or when this happened.

Moving from the Known to the Unknown
Whenever you study or teach, go from the known to

unknown. And if nothing is immediately known, do all you can to see *what can be known*.[3] Our times of biblical illiteracy in the United States of America are a reproach to a people whose founding fathers feared God and respected the Bible—and it is my passion and the passion of my colleagues at Precept Ministries International to turn this around by doing all we can to help people fall in love with the Word of God again and study it in a way that enables them to discover truth for themselves.

If you didn't know that the *who* in verse 5 are the people who were saved out of Egypt, the children of the sons of Jacob, whose name was changed to Israel (and you didn't have a Bible with good cross-references in the margin of the text), then you would start with what you know—what the text tells you: *Egypt*.

Using a concordance, you'd search the Bible for *Egypt*, beginning in Genesis and moving through book by book. Eventually you'd come to the following verses and learn what happened to the people who didn't believe God. Look these up and see what you learn. Record your insights next to the verses.

Exodus 12:40-51

---

3. If you use the New Inductive Study Series for personal devotions, you'll familiarize yourself with the Bible book by book. These are perfect for small group studies, family devotions, and Sunday school. In just 15 minutes a day, they'll take you from a milk to meat knowledge of the Word of God. For more information, go online to www.precept.org.

Numbers 14:29-32

1 Corinthians 10:1-11

Now then, we are not going to take this any further at this point since my purpose is to teach you the basics of how to study the Bible, and I only have a few days left. If you want to go deeper, we have a five-week Precept Upon Precept study on Jude and teaching tapes to go with it.

Ask Questions as You Study the Text

Read Jude 4-7 again to refresh your memory as to its content. It is good to read it aloud—hearing repeated readings will help store it in your memory bank.

As you already observed, Jude is supporting the judgment of these ungodly men by highlighting God's judgment in the past on ungodliness and the disobedience of unbelief.

Now let me show you the kind of questions you can ask to find out what the text says and means. Questions are very important in Bible study. Learn to ask them and to search out the answers in the text. Although some of the questions I am going to ask may seem redundant, answer them anyway. They will help you learn better.

- What two illustrations does Jude give in verses 6 and 7? List them and examine each by asking the pertinent 5 W's and an H: who, what, when, where, why and how. In this case, see if you can find out *who* is involved, *what* they did, *what* the consequences were (*how* did God respond?), *when* judgment will come, and *how* long it lasted (or will last). Record your answers.

- What truth does each illustration reinforce?

- What is the connection between the angels and Sodom and Gomorrah (and the cities around them)? What words give you the clue?

- Verse 7 says, "in the same way as *these*." Who do you think the "these" are? Why?

Let me remind you that all these questions will help you accurately interpret the text.

Does the *these* who "indulged in gross immorality" refer to the angels or the cities? If you can't identify *these,* where do you go from here? (The answer is important—if it refers to angels, you receive additional insight into the identity of the angels.)

If you cannot discern who *these* are from the structure of the sentence, one of the ways to find out is to use tools that help you with the original language. The tools will enable you to look up the gender of *angels* and *cities* to see if either matches the gender of *these.* If you were to do this, you would discover that the word *cities* (verse 7) is feminine, and *angels* (verse 6) is masculine. *These* is also masculine.

Since *these* seems to refer to the angels, you might ask what else the Scriptures teach about angels—and let Scripture interpret Scripture. So once again you would go to your concordance and search out the references to angels. Such an adventure would take you to some very interesting passages, such as 2 Peter 2, which is very similar to Jude.

Now, whatever you would decide on the identity of the angels, God makes it clear that Sodom and Gomorrah and the cities around them indulged in gross immorality in the same way that the angels did.

What happened to Sodom and Gomorrah and why? A study of Genesis would show you their sin was exceedingly grave (Genesis 18:20). Genesis 19 then gives you insight into their sin.

- Take a few minutes and read Genesis 18:16–19:29.

As you do, watch the references to *sin* and to sexual activity. What do you observe?

• According to the text of Scripture, what happens to Sodom and Gomorrah and why?

If you tie Genesis 18–19 with Jude 4-7, you see that *licentiousness* (lack of moral restraints, moral anarchy, and disregard for strict rules of correctness) is manifested in "gross immorality."

Forming Your Worldview

How needful this message is. Our culture is so complacent about morals today—we are a nation of adulterers and fornicators. People think nothing of living together before entering into the covenant of marriage. As a nation and as a church we're embroiled in controversies over the issues of what constitutes sex, immorality in many forms, and homosexuality and lesbianism.

Are such lifestyles acceptable? Should they be considered normal? Can people practice immorality—any form of sexual activity outside the bonds of marriage between a man and a woman—and be true children of God? Think about these things. Where are you going to stand? And will you stand?

Write out your convictions and commitment. Putting it in black and white can make a difference. It helps us solidify issues.

By the way, you just recorded your worldview on the issue. How biblical is it?

A worldview is the way you look at and analyze the culture. It's the lens through which you view the world—its morals and mores. Statistics show that very few Christians view the culture from a biblical perspective. Could it be because they either don't know how to study the Bible or don't study it? Or if they do, they may ignore the fact that the Bible has anything to do with the culture.

Oh, Beloved, this is why society is degenerating and the family and relationships are falling apart. We can't view the world biblically if we don't know the Bible! Thus we are left to our own desires, thoughts, or the current winds of philosophy, psychology, sociology, and liberal theology that does not hold to the inerrancy of the Bible.

Remember, people with a biblical worldview see things the way God sees them, think the way He thinks, and then adjust their lives accordingly.

Well, I've given you enough to think about today. Tomorrow we'll get back to the issue of identifying the angels who "indulged in gross immorality."

Day Twenty-Six

Using Commentaries

Yesterday we talked about the identity of the *those* in Jude who indulged in "gross immorality and went after strange flesh." What do you do when you have worked with the text as much as you can to dig out the answers, and you want to make sure you are on the right track? This is where commentaries come in.

Using Commentaries

After you study inductively, learning all you can on your own, you are prepared to turn to the works of others. You've done your own work; now you're more capable of appreciating the scholarly work of others and if necessary, sorting truth from error in their teachings and commentaries.

When listening to—or reading—the teaching of others, be sure to do several things:

- Compare what is said with the Word of God. Look up the reference the teachers quote and check the context.

- Make sure the teachers and commentators are solid and handle the text reputably.

- Know where they are coming from theologically. What is their bent doctrinally? Is this the perspective they are going to teach from? Will it color what they explain?

- Make sure the teaching is not based on an obscure passage. Doctrine should never be derived from a text that is difficult to understand or interpret. A rule of thumb: Never choose the obscure over the clear.

- Check out other reputable teachers and commentaries.

Those are some quick tidbits. If you want further insight on interpretation and commentaries, check out my *How to Study Your Bible.*

Now let's continue to see how to move through the text. When you study a book of the Bible and move through it chapter by chapter, watch the flow of thought. See how one verse connects with another and note when the author changes subjects. This helps you keep truth in context.

Everything in the Bible is written—and written in a certain way—for a reason. Your task is to discover the author's purpose—

> to discern his intent,
>
> to follow his flow of thought,
>
> to believe he says what he wants to say,
>
> to seek to understand exactly what he means,
>
> and to order your thoughts and life accordingly.

Therefore, let's begin by reading Jude 5-16. Look at every place you marked the references to the *ungodly*.

Did you notice the terms of comparison "just as" and "in

the same way as" in Jude 7? We mentioned comparisons earlier in this book, and I wanted you to see these. Now read Jude 8. It says "in the same way these men..."

- As you take this verse apart, make sure you identify who "these men" are in verse 8. Who are they?

- And with whom is Jude comparing them?

Leaving the illustration of the judgments of those mentioned in verses 5-7, Jude returns in verse 8 to describing the "ungodly persons who turn the grace of our God into licentiousness and deny our only Master and Lord, Jesus Christ."

- Are these ungodly persons dealing with reality or dreaming?

- List the three things these men—the ungodly—do by dreaming. Or to put it another way, what does the dreaming lead to?

When I see what I call a simple list in the text, I number the points right there where they are recorded. In Jude 8, I put a ①over "defile the flesh," a ②over "reject authority" and a ③over "revile angelic majesties." This way I can spot the three things quite easily and quickly.

Now, let's stop for a moment and think about this, Beloved. Do you dream about things you cannot have, things God has forbidden, relationships that are illegitimate? If so, you are being warned what *dreaming*—not keeping your thoughts under control, or as Paul puts it in 2 Corinthians 10:5, "taking every thought captive to the obedience of Christ"—can lead to if it goes unchecked. Beware!

Note what happens in verse 9.

- What repeated word ties verses 9-10 with verse 8?

- Did you notice in your observations that verses 9-10 begin with "but"? *But* is a term of contrast. What is being contrasted in verses 8-9?

- What is being contrasted in verses 9-10?

- By using Michael, the archangel, for an illustration against reviling angelic majesties, which is what the ungodly are doing, Jude teaches us something that is not revealed in any other place in the Word of God. You learn Michael and the devil had a contest over the body of Moses. Now that is interesting! By the way, I mark every reference to Satan, the devil, and all those under his domain who belong to the spirit world (evil spirits, demons, and principalities) with a red pitchfork like this ψ .

- Of course, when you have time, you might want to see what the Bible has to say about Michael the archangel.

In verses 11-12 you see again how Jude describes these men and their actions. You made a list of these things when you looked at all the places you marked *ungodly* men. Now is the time to get into the details of the text, and that we will do tomorrow.

Day Twenty-Seven

Application

As you move through the text, make sure you check out the details. When you read Jude 11 you quickly realize that if you are going to understand these ungodly men, you are going to have to have some insight into the way of Cain, the error of Balaam, and the rebellion of Korah. To gloss over these statements is to ignore the point God is trying to make.

Checking Out the Details

If you are going to understand the ungodly, your next step in Bible study would be to look up *Cain, Balaam,* and *Korah* and see what you can learn about...

- the *way* of Cain
- the *error* of Balaam
- the *rebellion* of Korah

You would look up *Cain, Balaam,* and *Korah* the same way you looked up *Egypt.* Don't go to a commentary; rather, get into that trusty concordance—paper or electronic—and go for it. You want to discover truth for yourself so you can discern truth from error. The process of digging out truth on your own will so broaden your knowledge of the Word of God and the God of the Word.

Figures of Speech

Look at verses 12-13 as Jude continues with his description of the ungodly. Watch the figures of speech—the metaphors—Jude uses to paint his verbal picture of these ungodly people.

A figure of speech is a word, a phrase, or an expression used in a figurative rather than literal sense. Metaphors and similes are figures of speech. A metaphor is an implied comparison, and a simile is a clearly stated one.

See how many metaphors are in verses 12-13, beginning with "hidden reefs." List them below.

If you are not familiar with figures of speech and how the Bible uses figurative language, once again let me refer you to one of three references: *How to Study Your Bible, Discover the Bible for Yourself,* or the *New Inductive Study Bible.*[4]

Read verses 14-16. Watch how Jude reaches back to the book of beginnings, Genesis, and the ministry of Enoch to let us know what the future holds for the ungodly.

---

4. You can find these in Christian bookstores or order them from Precept Ministries International.

Progressive Revelation

It's important that you understand the Bible is a *progressive* revelation. All the facts about events and persons are not always given at one time in one place. Enoch, in Jude 14, is a good example of this.

Read Genesis 5:18-24 and list what you observe about Enoch below.

Now read Jude 14-15 and list what you learn about Enoch.

Did you notice that although Enoch is mentioned in Genesis 5:18-24, Jude is the first to tell us of Enoch's prophecy about the Lord coming to judge the ungodly? Nothing is revealed about this prophecy until the second to last book of the Bible! This is one of many things that make Bible study an awesome, delightful adventure.

So many times my heart is filled with wonder as I watch how God weaves His truths together. I sit in amazement and find myself thanking Him over and over for the privilege we have to possess His Word and by His Spirit be able to see these things—to discover truth for ourselves by carefully observing the text.

My heart so often aches for those who miss treasures like this simply because they won't discipline themselves to study God's Word. They miss so much—including the pure joy of being taught by God Himself.

This, Beloved, is why you and I must study the whole counsel of God's Word, all 66 books.[5] Reason with me for a moment. Sixty-six books comprise the holy Scriptures. Apparently God thinks we need 66 books in order for us to be "adequate, equipped for every good work" (2 Timothy 3:17); otherwise He would have given us more or less. Therefore don't you think it is our responsibility as His children to know the content of these 66 books, which comprise the Bible? Aren't we to study them and handle them accurately so that we might be approved to God as 2 Timothy 2:15 says, so we won't be ashamed?

How are you doing, Beloved, in studying the content of the Bible? Not just reading it through, although that is commendable, but studying it carefully so you can handle it accurately?

And what will be our excuse when we see God face-to-face and give an account for our deeds as Christians (as 2 Corinthians 5:10 says) and tell Him we didn't have time to study His Word?

---

5. This is the reason God raised up Precept Ministries International—to establish people in God's Word. We exist to help people all over the world do this in their own language! It's such an incredible calling and ministry—one we want you to be involved in. We have the training and the tools to equip you—in person or online. Contact us at www.precept.org or write to us at Precept Ministries International, PO Box 182218, Chattanooga, TN 37422.

Now, Beloved, I want us to look at two more things before we call it a day.

First, Jude, the brother of Jesus, reminds us in verses 18-19 that the ungodly are the mockers that the apostles warned us of. Peter says the same thing in 2 Peter.

Do you and I need to know about these ungodly persons? The answer becomes obvious when you read Jude. These ungodly people were so on Jude's heart that he changed what he intended to write about and devoted most of his letter to a vivid description of them and of the judgment that awaits them.

Second and finally, I want us to talk about application.

Application

As a student of the Bible I need to ask myself what I am going to do with what I learned. How do I apply God's Word? As I mention in *How to Study Your Bible,* I believe that 2 Timothy 3:16-17 teaches us about application.

Paul tells us that Scripture is profitable for four things: teaching (doctrine), reproof (showing us where we are wrong), correction (showing us how to make the wrong right), and for training in righteousness (how we are to live according to His precepts, according to what God says is right).

Thus, after every period of study you might apply what you have read and studied by asking yourself questions like these:

- What have I been taught in this passage, and am I going to believe it and live according to this truth?

- Has God shown me anything that I am doing that is wrong?

- How can I right that wrong? What must I change or do in order to comply with the Word of truth?

- What have I learned about how I am to live? How can I put that into practice immediately?

Now then, Beloved student, why don't you bring today's study to a close by searching out the answers to several of these questions. Or if your study time is up, think on these things as you go about your day.

A Biblical
Systematic Theology

I am going to miss talking with you, for that is what I feel I have done as I've written this. It's hard to believe this is our final day together in this most noble quest. How I do pray I will hear from you. I want to know what God does in you and through you. I also know, Beloved, that what you learn is not just for you but also for you to share with others. Do you realize what would happen if those who claim His name, calling themselves Christians, would esteem His words more precious than their necessary food?

Our final day of study is going to focus on what Jude says to the called—the beloved in God the Father and kept for Jesus Christ.

And where do we begin? You know, don't you! In prayer. Why don't you get up and get down—down on your knees or on your face—and pour out your heart to God.

I saved Jude's comments to the "beloved" until now because Jude mentions them not only at the beginning of his letter but also at the end. Now you're ready to find out why.

Read through Jude aloud. Make sure you marked every

reference to the *recipients*. When you finish, look at every place in the text where you marked the references to the *beloved*. What do you learn about them—about you? Say it aloud. It is good to hear truth—to proclaim it with your lips! Speaking the truth helps it to stick in your mind.

Now read through the list you made on the *beloved*.

At some point in your study, you will probably want to go deeper—to get into the details and explore the words Jude uses to describe those to whom he's writing. You could begin with verse 1 and the word *called*.

This is an interesting way of identifying the recipients, isn't it? I wonder if anyone else does this? To find out the answer, where would you go? That's right! You would go to your concordance and look up *called*, see where it is used, check out its context, and see if that explains why they are *the called*. If you've never done this, you are going to be enlightened and encouraged. Being called by the Creator of the universe, the one and only true God, is an awesome thing.

Yet there is more to be discovered. Even though we are not going into the beauty and enlightenment that can come by knowing the tense, mood, and voice of verbs—that is in *How to Study Your Bible* or better still in William D. Mounce's book *Greek for the Rest of Us*—I want to take just a moment to show you a treasure you discover when you dig deeper.[6]

Beloved and *kept* in verse 1 are perfect passive participles. Knowing what this means can so enrich your understanding of how God views you.

The perfect tense indicates a past completed action with

---

6. Mounce's book, published by Zondervan, is about "Mastering Bible Study Without Mastering Biblical Languages." Precept Ministries International does a variety of teaching and training workshops across the United States and around the world in 67 languages. If you are interested in attending these or knowing what is available, go online to www.precept.org for more information.

a present or continuing result. Pause for a moment to digest that. Once you are His, you are beloved forever! The passive voice means the subject receives the action of the verb. So what does this mean practically? God is the one who declares you beloved. He is the one who keeps you! Stand in reverence, my friend—you are called by God, forever beloved and forever kept! Isn't that a treasure!

Now what does *kept* mean? Keep and kept are used in verses 1, 6, 21, and 24. The Greek word translated *kept* is *tereo* and means "to watch over" except in verse 24. In verse 24 the word translated *keep* is *phulasso*—"to guard by way of protection."

When you learn truths like this, take time to worship God in truth. Thank God for so great a salvation. Rehearse the truth and let it soak deep into your heart as you absorb it in faith. Sometimes we are so quick to embrace a lie about ourselves and so slow to embrace truth. Remember truth sanctifies you—it sets you apart from wrong and worldly thinking. This is why Romans 12:1-2 exhorts us to be transformed by the renewing of our minds.

Look for God's Instructions to His People

When you read the Word of God, notice the things our Lord God wants us to believe and consequently to do or to live in the light of. What are His instructions? When I read the Bible and come across an instruction, I often write the word *instruction* in the margin. You could do this or devise your own symbol for instructions. I've used a simple check mark, which reminds me to "check out" this instruction and make sure I am living according to it.

Read through Jude and in some way note the things Jude

wants his readers to do. Since he doesn't mention many, list them below.

Now, let's talk for a minute about what you observed. Jude's purpose for writing this epistle was a compelling one. He wanted the recipients to contend earnestly for the faith that was once for all delivered to us. "Contend earnestly" is in the present tense—it should be a habit of our Christian walk. This is the first instruction you come to.

Now look at the second instruction. It's in verse 17, near the end of the letter. Jude has told us why we should contend for the faith, and he has described those among us who creep in, professing to have faith but not possessing it, turning the grace of God into licentiousness, saying you can live any way you want, and denying our only Master and Lord, Jesus Christ.

Now Jude assures us of those persons' impending judgment. But he doesn't leave it there—he says you and I need to do something.

First, we need to remember what we learned about these people. Second, we need to keep ourselves in the love of God.

Keep is an aorist active imperative verb, which means it's a command.

Without knowing the tense, mood, and voice, you might not see that *keep* is a main verb supported by three participles: *building, praying,* and *waiting.* All are present participles, so they all call for habitual action.

If you didn't know the construction of the verb forms, could you still get the point? Yes. I am sure you listed *building, praying,* and *waiting.* Knowing the grammar just reinforces what you're learning and leads you further into the truth.

But is that the end of the instructions? No! Three more things follow in verses 22-23 as Jude draws our attention to three different situations and tells us how to handle them:

- Some people doubt—have mercy.
- Some people need a quick rescue—grab them as if they were falling into a fire. (They are!)
- Some people are really polluted! Be careful and maintain a holy fear so you aren't drawn into their sin!

That is a lot to think about, isn't it? What great and wise instructions. When we follow them, we bring God pleasure and reap the rewards and blessings of obedience.

A Biblical Systematic Theology

Finally, when you study any book of the Bible, you want to see what you learn about God the Father, about Jesus Christ, His Son, and about the Holy Spirit. This helps build your knowledge of the Godhead—to know the Father, Son, and Spirit and understand their ministry. See what Jude tells you about each.

God the Father	Jesus Christ	The Holy Spirit

You also want to review what you've learned about any specific subject dealt with in the text. This is the way you build a biblical systematic theology. You learn about the Father, the Son, and the Spirit or a particular person or subject by discovering what the Bible says as a whole on each topic or person. This is far more preferable than embracing a certain theological persuasion and then viewing all of Scripture from that perspective. Building a biblical systematic theology this way takes longer, but it's the better way, the higher way, for you are discovering truth for yourself.

Well, faithful one, you have persevered, and we have come to the end of our study. Oh, how I would love to sit and discuss Jude with you now that you have done this level of study. Think of how you have built yourself up in your most holy faith just this week, let alone over the last 28 days! Thank you, Beloved of God, for honoring our Father by honoring His Word. I say that with the deepest sense of love and gratitude. I know if you continue to study this way you surely will be able to say, "I have not turned aside from Your ordinances, for You Yourself have taught me" (Psalm 119:102).

> Now to Him who is able to keep you from stumbling, and to make you stand in the presence of His glory blameless with great joy, to the only God our Savior, through Jesus Christ our Lord, be glory, majesty, dominion and authority, before all time and now and forever. Amen.

Observation Worksheets

2 Kings 22

1 Josiah was eight years old when he became king, and he reigned thirty-one years in Jerusalem; and his mother's name *was* Jedidah the daughter of Adaiah of Bozkath.

2 He did right in the sight of the LORD and walked in all the way of his father David, nor did he turn aside to the right or to the left.

3 Now in the eighteenth year of King Josiah, the king sent Shaphan, the son of Azaliah the son of Meshullam the scribe, to the house of the LORD saying,

4 "Go up to Hilkiah the high priest that he may count the money brought in to the house of the LORD which the door keepers have gathered from the people.

5 "Let them deliver it into the hand of the workmen who have the oversight of the house of the LORD, and let them give it to the workmen who are in the house of the LORD to repair the damages of the house,

6 to the carpenters and the builders and the masons and for buying timber and hewn stone to repair the house.

7 "Only no accounting shall be made with them for the money delivered into their hands, for they deal faithfully."

8 Then Hilkiah the high priest said to Shaphan the scribe, "I have found the book of the law in the house of the LORD." And Hilkiah gave the book to Shaphan who read it.

9 Shaphan the scribe came to the king and brought back word to the king and said, "Your servants have emptied out the money that was found in the house, and have delivered it into the hand

of the workmen who have the oversight of the house of the LORD."

10 Moreover, Shaphan the scribe told the king saying, "Hilkiah the priest has given me a book." And Shaphan read it in the presence of the king.

11 When the king heard the words of the book of the law, he tore his clothes.

12 Then the king commanded Hilkiah the priest, Ahikam the son of Shaphan, Achbor the son of Micaiah, Shaphan the scribe, and Asaiah the king's servant saying,

13 "Go, inquire of the LORD for me and the people and all Judah concerning the words of this book that has been found, for great is the wrath of the LORD that burns against us, because our fathers have not listened to the words of this book, to do according to all that is written concerning us."

14 So Hilkiah the priest, Ahikam, Achbor, Shaphan, and Asaiah went to Huldah the prophetess, the wife of Shallum the son of Tikvah, the son of Harhas, keeper of the wardrobe (now she lived in Jerusalem in the Second Quarter); and they spoke to her.

15 She said to them, "Thus says the LORD God of Israel, 'Tell the man who sent you to me,

16 thus says the LORD, "Behold, I bring evil on this place and on its inhabitants, *even* all the words of the book which the king of Judah has read.

17 "Because they have forsaken Me and have burned incense to other gods that they might provoke Me to anger with all the work of their hands, therefore My wrath burns against this place, and it shall not be quenched."'

18 "But to the king of Judah who sent you to inquire of the LORD thus shall you say to him, 'Thus says the LORD God of Israel, "*Regarding* the words which you have heard,

19 because your heart was tender and you humbled yourself before

the LORD when you heard what I spoke against this place and against its inhabitants that they should become a desolation and a curse, and you have torn your clothes and wept before Me, I truly have heard you," declares the LORD.

20 "Therefore, behold, I will gather you to your fathers, and you will be gathered to your grave in peace, and your eyes will not see all the evil which I will bring on this place." '" So they brought back word to the king.

2 Kings 23:1-3

1 Then the king sent, and they gathered to him all the elders of Judah and of Jerusalem.

2 The king went up to the house of the LORD and all the men of Judah and all the inhabitants of Jerusalem with him, and the priests and the prophets and all the people, both small and great; and he read in their hearing all the words of the book of the covenant which was found in the house of the LORD.

3 The king stood by the pillar and made a covenant before the LORD, to walk after the LORD, and to keep His commandments and His testimonies and His statutes with all *his* heart and all *his* soul, to carry out the words of this covenant that were written in this book. And all the people entered into the covenant.

Jonah 1

1 The word of the LORD came to Jonah the son of Amittai saying,

2 "Arise, go to Nineveh the great city and cry against it, for their wickedness has come up before Me."

3 But Jonah rose up to flee to Tarshish from the presence of the LORD. So he went down to Joppa, found a ship which was going to Tarshish, paid the fare and went down into it to go with them to Tarshish from the presence of the LORD.

4 The LORD hurled a great wind on the sea and there was a great storm on the sea so that the ship was about to break up.

5 Then the sailors became afraid and every man cried to his god, and they threw the cargo which was in the ship into the sea to lighten *it* for them. But Jonah had gone below into the hold of the ship, lain down and fallen sound asleep.

6 So the captain approached him and said, "How is it that you are sleeping? Get up, call on your god. Perhaps *your* god will be concerned about us so that we will not perish."

7 Each man said to his mate, "Come, let us cast lots so we may learn on whose account this calamity *has struck* us." So they cast lots and the lot fell on Jonah.

8 Then they said to him, "Tell us, now! On whose account *has* this calamity *struck* us? What is your occupation? And where do you come from? What is your country? From what people are you?"

9 He said to them, "I am a Hebrew, and I fear the LORD God of heaven who made the sea and the dry land."

10 Then the men became extremely frightened and they said to him, "How could you do this?" For the men knew that he was fleeing from the presence of the LORD, because he had told them.

11 So they said to him, "What should we do to you that the sea may become calm for us?"—for the sea was becoming increasingly stormy.

12 He said to them, "Pick me up and throw me into the sea. Then the sea will become calm for you, for I know that on account of me this great storm *has come* upon you."

13 However, the men rowed *desperately* to return to land but they could not, for the sea was becoming *even* stormier against them.

14 Then they called on the LORD and said, "We earnestly pray, O LORD, do not let us perish on account of this man's life and do not put innocent blood on us; for You, O LORD, have done as You have pleased."

15 So they picked up Jonah, threw him into the sea, and the sea stopped its raging.

16 Then the men feared the LORD greatly, and they offered a sacrifice to the LORD and made vows.

17 And the LORD appointed a great fish to swallow Jonah, and Jonah was in the stomach of the fish three days and three nights.

Jonah 2

1 Then Jonah prayed to the LORD his God from the stomach of the fish,

2 and he said,
"I called out of my distress to the LORD,
And He answered me.
I cried for help from the depth of Sheol;
You heard my voice.

3 "For You had cast me into the deep,
Into the heart of the seas,
And the current engulfed me.
All Your breakers and billows passed over me.

4 "So I said, 'I have been expelled from Your sight.
Nevertheless I will look again toward Your holy temple.'

5 "Water encompassed me to the point of death.
The great deep engulfed me,
Weeds were wrapped around my head.

6 "I descended to the roots of the mountains.
The earth with its bars *was* around me forever,
But You have brought up my life from the pit, O LORD my God.

7 "While I was fainting away,
I remembered the LORD,
And my prayer came to You,
Into Your holy temple.

8 "Those who regard vain idols
   Forsake their faithfulness,

9 But I will sacrifice to You
   With the voice of thanksgiving.
   That which I have vowed I will pay.
   Salvation is from the LORD."

10 Then the LORD commanded the fish, and it vomited Jonah up onto the dry land.

Jonah 3

1 Now the word of the LORD came to Jonah the second time, saying,

2 "Arise, go to Nineveh the great city and proclaim to it the proclamation which I am going to tell you."

3 So Jonah arose and went to Nineveh according to the word of the LORD. Now Nineveh was an exceedingly great city, a three days' walk.

4 Then Jonah began to go through the city one day's walk; and he cried out and said, "Yet forty days and Nineveh will be overthrown."

5 Then the people of Nineveh believed in God; and they called a fast and put on sackcloth from the greatest to the least of them.

6 When the word reached the king of Nineveh, he arose from his throne, laid aside his robe from him, covered *himself* with sackcloth and sat on the ashes.

7 He issued a proclamation and it said, "In Nineveh by the decree of the king and his nobles: Do not let man, beast, herd, or flock taste a thing. Do not let them eat or drink water.

8 "But both man and beast must be covered with sackcloth; and let men call on God earnestly that each may turn from his wicked way and from the violence which is in his hands.

9 "Who knows, God may turn and relent and withdraw His burning anger so that we will not perish."

10 When God saw their deeds, that they turned from their wicked way, then God relented concerning the calamity which He had declared He would bring upon them. And He did not do *it*.

Jonah 4

1 But it greatly displeased Jonah and he became angry.

2 He prayed to the LORD and said, "Please LORD, was not this what I said while I was still in my *own* country? Therefore in order to forestall this I fled to Tarshish, for I knew that You are a gracious and compassionate God, slow to anger and abundant in lovingkindness, and one who relents concerning calamity.

3 "Therefore now, O LORD, please take my life from me, for death is better to me than life."

4 The LORD said, "Do you have good reason to be angry?"

5 Then Jonah went out from the city and sat east of it. There he made a shelter for himself and sat under it in the shade until he could see what would happen in the city.

6 So the LORD God appointed a plant and it grew up over Jonah to be a shade over his head to deliver him from his discomfort. And Jonah was extremely happy about the plant.

7 But God appointed a worm when dawn came the next day and it attacked the plant and it withered.

8 When the sun came up God appointed a scorching east wind, and the sun beat down on Jonah's head so that he became faint and begged with *all* his soul to die, saying, "Death is better to me than life."

9 Then God said to Jonah, "Do you have good reason to be angry about the plant?" And he said, "I have good reason to be angry, even to death."

10 Then the LORD said, "You had compassion on the plant for

which you did not work and *which* you did not cause to grow, which came up overnight and perished overnight.

11 "Should I not have compassion on Nineveh, the great city in which there are more than 120,000 persons who do not know *the difference* between their right and left hand, as well as many animals?"

Jude

1 Jude, a bond-servant of Jesus Christ, and brother of James, To those who are the called, beloved in God the Father, and kept for Jesus Christ:

2 May mercy and peace and love be multiplied to you.

3 Beloved, while I was making every effort to write you about our common salvation, I felt the necessity to write to you appealing that you contend earnestly for the faith which was once for all handed down to the saints.

4 For certain persons have crept in unnoticed, those who were long beforehand marked out for this condemnation, ungodly persons who turn the grace of our God into licentiousness and deny our only Master and Lord, Jesus Christ.

5 Now I desire to remind you, though you know all things once for all, that the Lord, after saving a people out of the land of Egypt, subsequently destroyed those who did not believe.

6 And angels who did not keep their own domain, but abandoned their proper abode, He has kept in eternal bonds under darkness for the judgment of the great day,

7 just as Sodom and Gomorrah and the cities around them, since they in the same way as these indulged in gross immorality and went after strange flesh, are exhibited as an example in undergoing the punishment of eternal fire.

8 Yet in the same way these men, also by dreaming, defile the flesh, and reject authority, and revile angelic majesties.

9 But Michael the archangel, when he disputed with the devil

and argued about the body of Moses, did not dare pronounce against him a railing judgment, but said, "The Lord rebuke you!"

10 But these men revile the things which they do not understand; and the things which they know by instinct, like unreasoning animals, by these things they are destroyed.

11 Woe to them! For they have gone the way of Cain, and for pay they have rushed headlong into the error of Balaam, and perished in the rebellion of Korah.

12 These are the men who are hidden reefs in your love feasts when they feast with you without fear, caring for themselves; clouds without water, carried along by winds; autumn trees without fruit, doubly dead, uprooted;

13 wild waves of the sea, casting up their own shame like foam; wandering stars, for whom the black darkness has been reserved forever.

14 *It was* also about these men *that* Enoch, *in* the seventh *generation* from Adam, prophesied, saying, "Behold, the Lord came with many thousands of His holy ones,

15 to execute judgment upon all, and to convict all the ungodly of all their ungodly deeds which they have done in an ungodly way, and of all the harsh things which ungodly sinners have spoken against Him."

16 These are grumblers, finding fault, following after their *own* lusts; they speak arrogantly, flattering people for the sake of *gaining an* advantage.

17 But you, beloved, ought to remember the words that were spoken beforehand by the apostles of our Lord Jesus Christ,

18 that they were saying to you, "In the last time there will be mockers, following after their own ungodly lusts."

19 These are the ones who cause divisions, worldly-minded, devoid of the Spirit.

20 But you, beloved, building yourselves up on your most holy faith, praying in the Holy Spirit,

21 keep yourselves in the love of God, waiting anxiously for the mercy of our Lord Jesus Christ to eternal life.

22 And have mercy on some, who are doubting;

23 save others, snatching them out of the fire; and on some have mercy with fear, hating even the garment polluted by the flesh.

24 Now to Him who is able to keep you from stumbling, and to make you stand in the presence of His glory blameless with great joy,

25 to the only God our Savior, through Jesus Christ our Lord, *be* glory, majesty, dominion and authority, before all time and now and forever. Amen.

THE *New* INDUCTIVE STUDY BIBLE

DISCOVERING THE TRUTH FOR YOURSELF

CHANGING THE WAY PEOPLE STUDY GOD'S WORD

"Inductive study of the Bible is the best way to discover scriptural truth...There is no jewel more precious than that which you have mined yourself."

—HOWARD HENDRICKS

Every feature is designed to help you gain a more intimate understanding of God and His Word. This study Bible, the only one based entirely on the inductive study approach, provides you with the tools for observing what the text says, interpreting what it means, and applying it to your life.

LORD

Teach Me to Pray

in 28 Days

KAY ARTHUR

KNOWING HOW TO PRAY CAN CHANGE YOUR LIFE

Many books offer tips on enhancing your prayer life—but they leave you adrift when it comes to actually praying. This 28-day study provides intensely practical insights to help you know *how* to pray, *what* to pray, and *what* to expect when you pray. Transform the way you pray (and live) today!

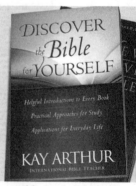